"ARE THEY SELLING HER LIPS?"

"ARE THEY SELLING HER LIPS?"

ADVERTISING AND IDENTITY

CAROL MOOG, PH.D.

William Morrow and Company, Inc.
New York

Copyright © 1990 by Carol Moog, Ph.D.

Recognizing the importance of preserving what has been written, it is the policy of William Morrow and Company, Inc., and its imprints and affiliates to have the books it publishes printed on acid-free paper, and we exert our best efforts to that end.

Library of Congress Cataloging-in-Publication Data

Moog, Carol.
  "Are they selling her lips?": advertising and identity / Carol Moog.
    p. cm.
  ISBN 0-688-08704-3
  1. Advertising—Psychological aspects.   2. Consumer behavior.
  I. Title.
  HF5822.M66 1990
  659.1'01'9—dc20   89-12965
                                                            CIP

Printed in the United States of America

First Edition

1 2 3 4 5 6 7 8 9 10

BOOK DESIGN BY JAYE ZIMET

Dedicated to my husband,
Roger,
and my daughter, Julie

ACKNOWLEDGMENTS

In a very real sense, this book is the product of philosophical and psychological issues I have explored throughout most of my personal and professional life. Along the way, I have been fortunate in finding teachers, friends, and colleagues who listened and provoked and challenged.

Early on in my forays into the world of advertising, I tracked down Walter Weir, advertising creative and author of *Truth in Advertising and Other Heresies*. I tried out ideas on him and picked his brain. He told me that if I had so much to say, I'd better start writing. It was one of the best pieces of advice I've ever gotten.

I will always be grateful to my friend and colleague George Gerbner, professor at the University of Pennnsylvania's Annenberg School of Communications and for many years its dean. George told me to forget trying to work with ad agencies. I took up the challenge and we've been exchanging ideas on advertising for years now. I thank him too for his reading and encouragement in the early stages of this book.

My agent, Jane Dystel, partner at Acton and Dystel, has been enormously helpful in many ways, not the least of which was introducing me to Ed Claflin. Ed's questions, comments, and editing contributed invaluably to the book. I thank Sherry Arden and Jennifer Williams for their editorial support and advice. Jim Donahue was consistently helpful. Jim Landis was an excellent creative resource in the final stages. My thanks to Cheryl Asherman for her superb jacket work, and to Nick Mazzella and Jaye Zimet for their caring and creativity in the designing of the book.

I'd like to thank the many friends and colleagues who were supportive and interested in talking through some of the book's ideas with me, especially Richard Hole, Mindy Goldberg, Sandy Malkin, Sarah Boote, Bob Boote, and Elizabeth de Vulpillières. Playing music with my "Blues Sister," Suzanne Gardner, always helped put things in perspective.

I thank my patients, who have allowed me to know them and help them and who, in turn, have helped me grow and know myself.

Not only has my husband, Roger, been his usual wonderful self throughout this writing, his critical reading and editorial comments made a real contribution to the book's integrity. My daughter, Julie, is an insightful, perceptive person in her own right, and her observations were consistently useful and interesting. And my parents' relentless energy for life has inspired my own.

For their thoughts and materials, I'd like to thank both the advertisers and ad agencies that are mentioned in the text and those whose contributions are reflected indirectly in the book, including Arian, Lowe & Travis Advertising, Inc.: Lee St. James, Daryl Travis; Balch Institute for Ethnic Studies: Gail Stern; BMW of North America: Richard Brooks; Chiat/Day: Sally Walsh, Patte Flaherty; Jacqueline Cochran, Inc.; Commodore International: Julie Bauer; DDB Needham Worldwide: Steven Swanson, Jack Mariucci, Bruce Delahorne; Doe-Anderson: Jay Giles; Gray Panthers: Maggie Kuhn, founder and national convenor; Jockey International: William C. Herrmann; Kirshenbaum & Bond: Jonathan Bond; Levine, Huntley, Schmidt & Beaver: Michael Moore; Lewis Gilman & Kynett: Bruce Berkowitz; Maidenform, Inc.: Bea Coleman, Marilyn Bane, Marcia Cacaci; Mandelbaum, Mooney & Associates: Ken Mandelbaum; Maryland Council for Developmental Disabilities: Katherine Hax; MTV (Music Television): Drana Prekelezaj, Barbara Kanowitz (formerly of MTV); Nissan Motor Corporation: Howard Rieder; Omni Publications International: Kathy Keeton, Marcia Potash; *Rolling Stone:* Leslie H. Zeifman; Scali, McCabe, Sloves, Inc.; Silo: Charles Jacoby; Smith Burke & Assam.

Special thanks to Donna Weiss and Sally Wetzler, CPA, for their contributions in time and openness. And to Bob Pottash, who first introduced me to the language of the unconscious in ads.

Finally, I'd like to thank my typist, Barbara Leibowitz, for her unfailing reliability and availability in preparing this manuscript.

CONTENTS

"ARE THEY SELLING HER LIPS?"

INTRODUCTION

My fascination with the power of advertising stems from a horrifying conclusion I came to when I was about ten years old.

I was glued to the TV, watching a commercial that had caught my attention. The woman on the screen was enthusiastically selling refrigerators. But I didn't care about refrigerators. My attention was riveted on the way she walked. I noted how she carefully placed one foot in front of the other. And what I concluded from watching that commercial was that I'd have to learn a whole new way of walking in order to be a grown-up.

Years later, I began to understand the real significance of that moment. In the intervening years, I had gotten my Ph.D. in psychology and worked extensively as a clinician and consultant. I had also become a mother. One day I was watching TV with my then five-year-old daughter, Julie. She was staring at the big, red, pouting mouth of a made-for-TV model imploring us to "taste the freshness."

Julie turned to me and asked, "Are they selling her lips?"

It dawned on me that advertisers sell toothpaste to adults. But to children—and the child in all of us—they sell how to look, how to act, how to be. I became concerned about the impact ads had on people's self-concept, not only as a psychologist, but as the mother of a growing little girl whose idea of who she was and who she was supposed to be was going to be inevitably influenced by Madison Avenue models persuading her to *be* like them as well as *buy* like them.

My experience with Julie fueled my drive to understand what

our psychological interactions with advertising are all about.

Since my undergraduate days, when I majored in philosophy, I've been interested in how people, emotionally and intellectually, sort out what is real for themselves—how individual perspectives on reality are processed. I was, and am, fascinated by the incredible variety of interpretations people give to projective test materials, such as Rorschach's inkblots, interpretations derived from *projecting* their own perceptions, perceptions drawn from the way each filters the world through his own screens of experience and personality. In a way, the world *is* a Rorschach. In a way, so is an ad.

People's perceptions of ads are colored by the same psychological issues and dynamics that they bring to bear on any other information the environment sends their way. I began to study the application of my longstanding interest in projective testing, the workings of the unconscious, Jungian archetypes, and semiotics (the systematic decoding of cultural signs and symbols) as a way of unraveling the psychological processes at work in advertising.

At the same time I was studying advertising, I was beginning to build my private practice. As I looked at the *products* that were being marketed, I became more aware of how these products were integrated into my patients' own searches for identity. I realized that *my* media awareness made me more closely attuned to the signals that they were giving off.

It was more than body language. It was a kind of *product language.*

A woman I will call Amy gave me a clue as to how product language might have a direct effect on the work that went on in therapy. A lawyer in her late twenties, Amy is definitely an A-type—highly motivated, compulsive, and attractive. A recent breakup with her longtime fiancé had thrown her into a depression. Fortunately, she has both a sense of humor and a good deal of perspective, which gave her the ability, at times, to laugh at herself.

During one of these moments, she gave a big sigh and said, "This is great. Here I am—the Pepsi generation—and I feel like jumping out the window."

It was natural for me to ask her, "Amy, what's the Pepsi generation all about?"

"Oh, you know—the old screaming over Michael Jackson bit. People going crazy. Having fun."

"Do you know anybody like that?"

"Not really," she said, "that's just the point. I missed all that. I started seeing Norm (her ex-fiancé) in college. When we weren't studying, we had these quiet little movie dates. I'd like to turn back the clock. I never got wild over anything."

"Come alive!" I said.

"Right." She smiled. "Come alive."

The moment passed, and the subject of "the Pepsi generation" dropped from our conversation.

But not from Amy's mind.

An image had been planted—the image of beautiful, happy, sexy young people running, dancing, and shouting with joy. The whole Pepsi campaign—one of the most high-powered and effective advertising campaigns in recent television history—had succeeded perfectly in achieving the desired psychological impact. It had made at least one young woman (and how many millions more?) long for the excitement and fun of a *new* generation—a generation that didn't slog through law school, work twelve-hour days, or break up with fiancés.

Amy had never seen the Pepsi generation in real life. She had never surrounded herself with the bottle-popping, Pepsi-sipping revelers she saw in those commercials. She would never stand in line all night for tickets for Michael Jackson, or anybody else. But the reality didn't matter. Those commercials existed on a plane of experience where she *wished* to be.

Amy wanted to be somewhere else. She wanted to be *someone* else. She wanted to stop being Amy and become part of the Pepsi generation, where life was less lonely, less frightening, and less demanding than the life she was living right now. Those brilliant commercials that were intended to make people like Amy thirsty for Pepsi were *actually* making people like Amy thirsty for a fantasy of life.

To what degree did the image of a perfect, joyous existence contribute to Amy's misery? Or, conversely, how much was she able to escape *into* that fantasy to help ease the pain she was feeling at that time? These questions are far too complex for statistical answers. But as I have become more alert to the product language of my clients, I have become increasingly certain that the impact is very real and very pervasive.

As I thought about Amy's and others' experiences, it was natural that I also began to wonder how those ads got created—how decisions were made—and whether advertisers were aware of what their ads were saying and how they worked on people. I wanted to get inside and learn how the whole thing operated. I also naïvely believed that my knowledge and perspective as a practicing psychologist—trained in both child and adult development!—would be immediately embraced by the advertising industry.

The fantasied welcome didn't happen exactly the way I'd imagined. I had blithely marched into a foreign country speaking the language of psychological dynamics and symbolic meanings. I encountered a tribe speaking the language of profits and conjuring ways of exorcising the dread demon of "clutter." (Clutter is the euphemism for the staggering fact that we are bombarded with between four-hundred and three-thousand advertising messages every day—too much for even that most cherished instrument of consumer revenge and power, the remote-control TV zapper, to eliminate.)

I had approached the advertising culture in alien clothes, speaking a peculiar dialect. Advertisers aren't in the business of making people feel better about themselves, they're in the *selling* business. If an ad is irritating, insulting, or abrasive enough to cut through the clutter and make an impact on the consumer, psychological sensitivity is irrelevant. Sales spell success.

So I got smarter. I got the training and experience I needed to translate my skills and knowledge into the more acceptable way psychologists are packaged to play the ad game. I shelved my role as a skeptic in the halls of the believers and developed proficiency as a market researcher. Among other ways of exploring the consumer psyche, a market researcher runs focus groups. So I learned how to gather together small groups of targeted consumers (and potential consumers) and ferret out (in creative, indirect ways—often using techniques derived from projective testing!) how they feel about products, ideas, and advertising concepts.

This approach worked a lot better as a way to get my foot in the door. In the agencies, I was properly clothed as a market researcher and was then able to communicate with business deci-sion-makers, and with those who are known in agency parlance as "the creatives." Appropriately dressed and packaged (my con-sultancy is named Creative Focus), I gained entry into the tribe and started learning more about its unique customs.

How does Madison Avenue see us? Agencies and advertisers spend an extraordinary amount of time and a truly staggering amount of money trying to figure out as much as they can about the needs of their target market. They want to know fantasies, buying be-havior, income, and insecurities so they can *position* their product in such a way as to make it absolutely irresistible. They hold focus groups, conduct surveys, and run pretests and posttests of com-mercials. Hours of presentations are made, and oceans of reports are written. Their findings and recommendations clearly point to the kind of advertising that should work best for a certain product with a specific target market of consumers (us).

You might well wonder what happens to all these reports gath-ered in order to help the writers and artists who create ads—I know I did.

They get filed. Not always—but regularly. Product managers, account executives, and research directors usually read executive summaries, while creatives often murmur something about not liking to "wade through reports." Then they go off to create ads based on a combination of their own intuition, their interpretation of the market researcher's stand-up presentation, and their expe-rience and knowledge about the product. It wasn't unusual for some clients to send me background material for a research project that contained an excellent, relatively recent report of findings on the very questions I was asked to explore.

I remember in particular one market-research director of a large company who asked me to study the psychological effectiveness of their advertising for a new deodorant. Now deodorant is one of those low-interest products that has about as much inherent excitement as banks, and inspires the same kind of inertia in its consumers. For people to change banks, and deodorants, they either have to be very, very unhappy with the product, or some-thing truly novel has to come up and clobber them with its su-periority.

Unfortunately for my client, there was absolutely nothing unique

about the company's "new" deodorant. Just another, not especially attractive, package on the shelf. Hadn't the wisdom of introducing this product already been researched by this giant
corporation? Didn't they have consumer studies on deodorant usage
that already answered their advertising questions?

After some digging, my requests for background information
landed me a box of reports, among which was a fairly recent study
of consumers' reactions to my clients' deodorant concepts. Not
surprisingly, the consultant concluded that, without anything different in form or function, the new deodorant ideas were headed
for oblivion. Not surprisingly, the findings of this report headed
for oblivion even faster. Furthermore—and this is amazing to
me—my client wanted me to go ahead with my study of the advertising effectiveness of a product that never should have been in
the first place.

So how do advertising decisions get made? Research is often
lip service at the altar of objectivity, while decisions are made in
response to the most powerful voices within an agency. If the
creative director of an agency doesn't agree with the research—if
it contradicts his or her intuition and clutter-cutting concepts—
it's the research that often gets shelved. If the advertiser's CEO
(or spouse) is shown a series of commercials and one particularly
strikes his or her fancy, chances are that's the one that gets produced. In the midst of all this, agencies are in an especially tough
position. If the product sells like mad, it's because of the advertiser's genius; if it bombs, it's the fault of the lousy agency, which
then gets fired.

Working on behalf of the advertising agency, I'm often used
as a bridge between creative and research. I translate report language into concrete images of what people like and don't like and
why they feel the way they do—which makes sense to creatives
responsible for advertising design. And I unravel the different levels
of meanings ads carry in their verbal and nonverbal language of
words and pictures. Once in a while, writers or artists are personally skittish about a psychologist looking too closely at their
creative work. But mostly, when they've seen how much they end
up learning about the messages they're actually sending, we've
ended up as creative partners. Sometimes I help agencies win ac-

counts or develop new ideas by analyzing competitors' brand personalities.

Working with advertisers, the people who produce and market the product, is sometimes a different story. At times, I've even been brought in as a kind of intellectual hired gun to help the advertiser articulate what he doesn't like, or what isn't working in the advertising. Sometimes I'm asked to analyze *why* a spectacularly successful campaign is working, so the agency can capitalize on its power and produce more and even better creative pool-outs (new commercials playing on the same idea). Advertisers ask me to help them develop a clear identity in the crowded marketplace of brand images, and I study symbols and the psychology of their consumers to map out the terrain. For me, the most exciting work happens when I'm part of an agency/advertiser team and advertising gets developed that sometimes manages to be psychologically positive for consumer psyches and product sales alike.

With this book, I'm the ad-watcher again, but an infinitely better informed one. I've returned as a skeptic in the halls of the believers, a mirror-breaker in a world of illusions. Advertising continues to be endlessly fascinating for me. I love the creativity. I like the complexity of the game. I'm intrigued by the psychological and ethical issues.

For those of you who feel victimized by the game—don't. Advertisers don't hold all the cards. So here's a look in the mirror, through the mirror, and behind the mirror. If you see yourself in there somewhere, watching them watching you watching them watching you, don't be alarmed. It's just part of the game.

CHAPTER 1

MEDIA MIRRORS

Breasts.
Philip Roth yearned for them.
Hef built an empire on them.
But Maidenform made the fortune from them.

Sharon, the forty-seven-year-old wife of a dentist with two grown children, is telling me about the dream she had three nights before:

> Richard and I were in a restaurant. I think it was the Citadel, where we ate about a month ago—I don't know. But it was different. There were all these men around, and I felt uncomfortable. But they weren't alone. They were there with some old women—like their mothers or grandmothers or something. And I was very angry at Richard. I remember fighting with him there before too. He kept telling me to shut up, that I was drinking too much. Suddenly, I realized I didn't have anything on and he was mad at me because everyone was staring. I thought, I've got to get out of here. I panicked. But I couldn't move. No one at the other tables seemed to pay any attention. And here's where it got really strange. I started to relax. I felt beautiful. And Richard smiled.

Sharon's dream has triggered a thought in my mind that starts to crystallize into an image that helps me understand what she's thinking about. I'm imagining Bea Coleman and her mother, Ida Rosenthal, and the brilliant campaign they launched more than thirty years ago. A campaign so brilliant that it touched the most potent fantasies of a woman's dreams.

It was the Maidenform fantasy. The "I dreamed I was . . . in my Maidenform bra" campaign ran for twenty years and made Bea Coleman and Ida Rosenthal rich beyond their wildest dreams.

The original Maidenform ads were created by the agency of Norman, Craig and Kummel Advertising, and showed women acting out fantasies (frequently controversial fantasies), that fully displayed their Maidenform bras. Ads like the lady lawyer who "dreamed I swayed the jury in my Maidenform bra" unleashed and exposed the secret fantasies of traditional women of the fifties and invited them to step brazenly into dreams of power and influence. What the ads had women "dream" was that they could go ahead and be exhibitionistic, but not just about their bodies; about their capabilities. Clearly, a psychological chord was struck with this campaign. Women sent scores of unsolicited photos of themselves in endless scenes of "I dreamed I was . . . in my Maidenform bra." One priceless example was Diamond Lil, accom-

panied by a letter from her daughter. In terms of how the campaign portrayed women, it was a real set-breaker. The campaign put the company on the map and gave cultural approval to powerful wishes women certainly harbored but rarely advertised.

What was going on in Diamond Lil and all the other women who responded so positively to the Maidenform campaign? This was pre–women's lib, when gender roles were still plainly spelled out: Females were Devoted Housewives and males were Preoccupied Breadwinners. Then along comes Maidenform with full-color photos of poised, clear-eyed, confident women unabashedly exposing their fantasies along with their chests. They're not in the least self-conscious. They're relaxed and composed. The campaign offered a sensational subconscious release for Diamond Lil and the duty-bound women of that period. It was enormously gratifying to identify with the courage of the Maidenform woman daring to show herself as fully developed to anyone interested in looking. Interested persons included parents, husbands, clergymen, and teachers. The fifties woman got to vicariously thumb her nose at all the right people. She got to break out of the socially appropriate straitjacket she'd willingly donned—ostensibly for the good of family and cultural stability—and try on a new identity.

Psychologically, that's what dreams are about anyway. They're what the unconscious produces, busily fulfilling wishes that our rational selves have deemed too outrageous to express in real life. There's something else about dreams. They show us images of ourselves that we've already accepted internally but that we haven't risked trying out yet.

I see the "I dreamed . . ." campaign as a kind of emotional road map for the women's lib activities that came to the surface in the seventies. Phyllis is the only woman I know who actually, ceremoniously, *burned* a bra—and if I told her that she could thank Maidenform for helping her get a picture of herself as an independent person, she'd have been furious. But like it or not, the campaign set the stage for Phyllis and the other women of her generation. Women interacted with the ads in spite of themselves because they were already gearing up for the kind of real-life dreams they made happen when the feminist movement took hold.

The "I dreamed I took the cue in my Maidenform bra" ad is a prime example of the kind of ad that could get to Phyllis, re-

CHANSONETTE shapes and supports your figure naturally

I dreamed I took the cue in my maidenform bra

gardless of her conscious protests. When a woman already fantasizing about being less inhibited reads the line "I dreamed I took the cue . . . ," she's already projecting herself into the picture. She's already hooked into seeing herself taking charge in what was traditionally a male-dominated situation. Not only does she take the cue stick, but she proceeds to handle it in a deft behind-the-back maneuver, all without losing a trace of her sultry femininity. The fantasy was powerful but safe. Although Phyllis would never admit it, it was perfectly congruent with women's needs at that time to stay feminine while getting strong. At the same time, the campaign helped women picture having power and control far outside the domestic domain.

Here was a landmark campaign that came at precisely the right time to rivet women's attention. A piece of anatomical support empowered their dreams, permitting them to become "Maidenform women," in control of themselves, their circumstances, and their future. The Maidenform campaign was a strong one, largely because it reflected one advertiser's personal convictions. Bea Coleman, Maidenform's dynamic CEO, always admired her entrepreneurial mother, Ida Rosenthal, who founded the company with her physician-husband, William. Ida was a powerhouse. Mother and daughter both dared to dream big and do more. The "I dreamed . . ." concept was turned down by another lingerie company but embraced by Maidenform, perhaps because it was consistent with both Bea's and Ida's perceptions of women. Bea seemed to use her mother as a positive role model, and Ida may have unintentionally modeled aspects of herself through the endless permutations of the dream campaign. She persuaded women not just to buy $100 million worth of underwear, but to see themselves as more capable people.

But the dream campaign hit social forces beyond its control—and turned with the tide of change. By the late sixties, the younger women who should have been buying Maidenform bras had begun to associate "I dreamed . . ." images with their mothers—and bras themselves with the constraints of traditional female roles and functions. When young women started ditching their bras along with their mothers' ideas as they reached for autonomy, the advertiser responded to the psychological climate by ditching the "I dreamed . . ." campaign. (Interestingly, Bea Coleman's own story runs a close parallel to the course of the campaign—this was just about the time that she shocked the male-dominated intimate-apparel industry in 1968 by taking over the company as president after her husband's death.)

What happened? Like Bea Coleman herself, women weren't just acknowledging their dreams of power, they were out there making them happen. The dream campaign symbolized the exciting but frustrated longings of the past. These were fantasy ads meant for the women they were trying to escape in their mothers and in themselves. The ads no longer had their initial freeing effect. Instead, they waved a red flag. Women like my old friend Phyllis were burning their bras, not dreaming about showing them off.

The Maidenform woman was mothballed for eleven years. When she reappeared, she launched the greatest controversy in bra history. In a reincarnation created by the Daniel & Charles advertising agency, she was still depicted doing active, even aggressive things, like commuting to work, reading *The Wall Street Journal,* going to the theater, or being a lawyer. She was daringly clad in her matching bra and panties. But now *there were men in the picture!* They appeared disinterested, oblivious to the delectable spectacle of "The Maidenform Woman. You never know where she'll turn up." The men were shot slightly out of focus. They were deeply absorbed, eyes discreetly everywhere else but you-know-where.

Here was a real twist, and the campaign ended up generating the kind of hot attention that left feminists seething and Maidenform sales soaring. Completely unanticipated! Maidenform didn't intend (as many advertisers do) to create a potentially explosive campaign. The agency just thought it had a great new approach for a new age. Advertiser and agency were equally surprised when the campaign got scorching reviews from angered members of women's movement. It also put Maidenform in the painful position of having to reevaluate the "success" of a campaign that, without question, was a success in terms of sales.

What ticked off women when Maidenform tried to turn them on? As the advertiser sees it, the campaign was inadvertently suggesting that the Maidenform woman had achieved her enviable position, such as tiger tamer, strictly on the basis of her sexuality rather than her actual competence. The most noteworthy clunker, the one that finally deep-sixed the "You never know where she'll turn up" campaign, was the white-coated lady doctor piece. Everyone (male or female) who had ever worn a white coat— nurses, lab technicians, beauticians, the American Medical Association —bombarded Maidenform with calls and letters of protest.

As the mail indicated, there were some obvious reasons why this campaign caused the uproar it did. With a female doctor exposing herself in a patient's hospital room, women's lib took a giant step backward. "Strip off the professional cover," these ads seemed to be saying, "and what you'll find is just another sex object."

At the time this campaign got started, however, I thought it would have upset people for an entirely different unconscious reason. I showed the ad to some of my colleagues and just asked their opinions of it. Mark, a Ph.D. psychologist who's been practicing about as long as I have, came up with what turned out to be the consensus:

"That's going to be one angry lady!"

"Okay," I asked, "why?"

Mark pointed to the two samples I'd shown him—the woman in the tiger cage and the doctor ad—and noted, "Look at the men in the pictures. Here's a woman with her clothes off, and they aren't paying any attention to her at all."

Mark and the others confirmed my own sense of the underlying problem. The most insulting thing about the ads was not that the woman had exposed herself—even in a professional role. That might have been intellectually offensive—yes, it could be demeaning to women who were rising in their professions—but it didn't explain the strength of the emotional reactions women had to the ads.

What was really most offensive were the self-indulgent, narcissistic posturings of the *men* in the picture. For the woman wearing a Maidenform bra, the experience was no longer a good dream. It was a bad dream. It is humiliating on the deepest levels, where our feelings of self-worth are most fragile, for any of us to expose ourselves at our most naked and vulnerable . . . and make no impact whatsoever. Women can easily identify with the Maidenform image in the ads, put themselves in her position and feel the angry confusion of someone who dolls herself up but still gets ignored.

There's more. Despite being pictured in the trappings of power, this Maidenform woman ended up looking weak and vulnerable. Look at the contrast between the unblinking confidence and forward-thrusting body posture of the lady pool-shark and check out the demure, downcast glance and tight-kneed toe-tipped stance of the tiger tamer. Maidenform tried to tell women that it was listening, that it respected their hard-won accomplishments, but it sent some subtle messages that undercut the communication. Women bought the bras but were left with images of themselves as "sweet nothings"—ironically the name of one of Maidenform's best-selling lines.

After four years of profitable (although sometimes uncomfortable) campaigning, Maidenform pulled back from its big-strong-pretty young-things-turning-up-half-naked-in-front-of-self-involved-men approach. Romance, Maidenform perceived, was coming back. It was time to turn from power to syrup. Women were beginning to gag on advertisers' endless portraits of them as superhuman jugglers of kids, career, hubby, and housework.

Stripped of any power cues, the next Maidenform Woman was one who "Dares to Dream." And what are her daring dreams about now? Sitting around wearing underwear and a wistful, vacant expression, she boldly fantasizes about going out on a date. Here is a woman with no pretensions of being anything other than the lovely, compliant, and ever-so-feminine creature her mother modeled in the fifties. She's straight out of the whistle-clean Harlequin Romance series, right down to the quasi–book-jacket logo in the corner. And like these little stories, Maidenform declares that its "Delectables" will "make your life as soft and smooth as your dreams."

At this stage of the game, all of us, women especially, have gotten to be fairly sophisticated cynics. We know that advertisers run various images of us to see whether they can stir a ripple of salesworthy responses. The "Dares to Dream" campaign reached out to women who had been feeling like miserable failures for fantasizing about guys. While everybody else was out there self-actualizing into steel-plated CEOs, Maidenform gave the "new romantics" permission to go ahead and dream the dreams of adolescent girls if they wanted.

Sales proved that many women wanted just that. Enough battling against male indifference and resistance. Maidenform was tired of trying to tickle the fancies of feminists; the campaign regressed to the lowest-risk imagery for the masses—woman as a glowworm for love.

While it clearly qualifies as a fluff piece, Wyse Advertising's "Dares to Dream" campaign is surpassed in regressiveness by its next series of "lifestyle" ads. "The Maidenform Woman. Today she's playful," whisks our heroine backward in time until she's a prepubescent who gets kind of emotional, but that's okay, because Maidenform will "fit" her "every move and mood" so she can stay just as cute as she is now. She's not even old enough to think about

The Maidenform Woman.
Today she's playful.

guys—"frisky as a kitten," "Today she's playful."

Now, no angry letters spewed forth on the heels of "Today she's playful." Whom *did* this appeal to? Well, there's Liz. She's very bright and possesses an MBA, which she sometimes waves over a conversation like a silk scarf—something to be admired but not used. She's surrounded by working friends, but she's filled her life with tennis and shopping and lunches. I like Liz, and it's over one of these lunches that she says to me, "I feel like having a temper tantrum."

I can't help thinking about how Liz creates herself in the image of the "Today she's playful" ad—defining herself not in terms of what she's accomplishing, but by her moods. Does Liz know what she's doing? I don't think so. Did the agency know what it was doing? I don't think so. Both are just creating what they hope are pretty pictures.

Where do you go with this? Unfortunately, Liz will probably just continue to be the subject of her moods. Maidenform wasn't quite so stuck—it changed agencies.

Following this purely saccharine retreat from Maidenform's gutsy heritage, the sixty-five-year-old lingerie company set out in pursuit of the Holy Grail of advertising—a new image. After a grueling selection process, Levine, Huntley, Schmidt & Beaver won the account—and the opportunity to sweat its way toward a singularly brilliant advertising idea.

What Levine, Huntley, Schmidt & Beaver created, and what the advertiser had the courage to appreciate, is a radical departure for lingerie ads.

No women, no product—just male movie-star-types like Omar Sharif, Michael York, and Corbin Bernsen. The campaign has been noticed by the media, by competitors, and apparently by women, who've written comments to the advertiser like "I don't normally watch commercials—however, your Michael York commercial is fantastic! So much so I've switched to Maidenform." "Your commercial will be shown at our annual meeting . . . as a prime example of excellent advertising. It appeals to women as adults, not children

. . . keep up the good work." And "This is the type of commercial that instills a need in me to purchase your product."

Now just what is driving these ads? What happens when women see someone like Omar Sharif shot in deep shadows, murmuring, "Lingerie says a lot about a woman. I listen as often as possible"? There's an edge of the forbidden, the dangerous, to Sharif's exotic, rakish seductiveness that is a psychological turn-on to the dainty dreamers of Maidenform's recent past. They can rebel against the sweet-young-thing image, and run away (in their fantasies) with a sexy devil. No one has to fake the modesty of a woman publicly displayed in her underwear. Sharif's appeal is also clearly to a mature market; he's not exactly the current heartthrob of younger women. So the advertiser moved away from charming vignettes of moody little models and is effectively hooking grownups with male bait.

With Corbin Bernsen of *L.A. Law*, the psychological lure isn't just juicy evil. Here's a recognizably competent lady-killer, who enters the mysterious realm of a lingerie department and finds it "a little embarrassing. A little intimidating." What a gift to the female ego! If Maidenform can give women a way to embarrass and intimidate the likes of Mr. Bernsen, even "a little,"

it's not just underwear anymore—it's personal power.

The story of women's relationship with Maidenform's images reflects the complex interactions we all have with advertising. Advertisers have to communicate with as large a group of us consumers as possible, but in reality, the communication is always one-to-one. Maidenform's first "I dreamed I . . ." campaign was a success because the fantasy it promoted matched the underlying aspirations of enough individuals to make up a mass market. The advertiser gave a big push to a hoop already rolling out the kitchen door of convention, but things changed when the fantasy of sexual power turned to the reality of political and social power.

Then Maidenform held up concrete images of strong women to try to keep up with all the changes. The trouble came when the advertiser unwittingly introduced doubts and insecurities with its "You never know where she'll turn up" series and women felt a bit as though they'd bought a measure of male indifference along with Maidenform's dream images. The advertiser responded by attempting to soothe its buyers with pictures of romantic security. And finally it courts its market with its latest put-yourself-in-the-picture invitations offered by dashing male sex objects.

The promise is still largely romance. But a woman isn't just faced with relating to an image of herself; now, she's asked to relate to her idea of a man's image of her. For this to work for Maidenform, a woman has to have enough self-confidence to imagine that she is the object of these lingerie lovers' underwear fantasies. It would work for Liz, but not for Ann. Ann's a nice woman who feels fat and unattractive and prefers to undress in the dark. These ads make her feel worse because she *can't* imagine herself in them. She flunks the fantasy test.

Maidenform's current strategy works for one other important reason—it sidesteps the question faced by all lingerie advertisers: How can you show a woman in her underwear without making her look either like an idiot or a slut? Most answers bomb.

Jockey International's ad for its line of female undergarments is a superb example of what can go wrong when a sincere desire to show real people using a product in believable ways is taken to extremes. The decision to profile Lynne Pirie, "Physician, Surgeon, Sports Medicine Specialist, Medical Director at North Phoenix Health Institute, Author/Lecturer," in her underwear was not an effort to

tap the superwoman segment of
the market, according to Jockey's
vice-president of advertising and
sales-promotion director. Despite
Dr. Pirie's list of credentials,
Jockey intended to personalize the
garment as worn not just by models but by the woman next door.

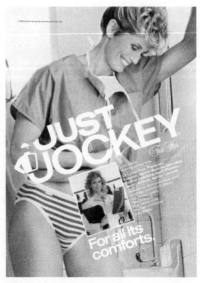

Jockey apparently overlooks
the skepticism inherent in the
woman's market. The image of a
certifiably successful stereotype
hoisting up her scrub suit the way
a little girl might show off her
new panties comes across as being
silly at best, insulting at worst. The advertiser and its agency,
Campbell-Mithun, made a conscious effort to design an ad that
would distinguish itself from the usual lingerie executions. But
there's no real difference between Jockey's girlish good doctor and
Maidenform's vaguely moronic "Today she's playful."

Advertisers have contrived numerous ways to harness women's
buying power. They have attempted to portray women deftly mas-
tering the roles of superlover, supercook, superprofessional, su-
permom, superartist, supergardener, and superhousekeeper. Most
flopped under the jaded stares of women consumers. Michelob's
late "Who says you can't have it all?" campaign offered us a "full-
time model and part-time business student" who studied "until
two in the morning" and had to be "on a shoot three hours later."
While it is certainly true that this woman might enjoy a beer at
the end of her marathon day, the majority of women don't feel as
if they have it all under such circumstances; they feel as if they're
losing their marbles.

Spiegel served up a casual family portrait of CEO/pilot/mom
("I've successfully managed one aviation company, two children
and three languages") with son and personal jet to promote
catalog use.

By and large, women have become pretty savvy to this kind
of hype. But what's in it for those who believe the image? The ad
holds up a mirror of who they're not, of what they aren't achieving.

Measured by Madison Avenue, most women would fall short. But we all know we're not just talking about women.

When can we laugh off the image—and when do we mistake the myth for reality?

Beverly is an art director. She works with images all the time, and knows just how advertising tries to work on her. And she's fought hard to maintain her independence—to be herself. But I hear her talk about her friends, and she always ends up compar-

"HOW I FOUND ALEXANDER JULIAN, NORMA KAMALI AND LIZ CLAIBORNE AT 40,000 FEET"

ing *them* to some famous face: "Oh, you know her, she looks like Cheryl Tiegs." And when I ask her whom *she* looks like, Beverly glances down and shrugs, "Oh, nobody, just plain old me."

Everybody struggles to develop a sense of security, a sense of personal identity. But most of us end up constantly glancing around to see if we measure up to those around us—and that includes supercharged media models. We hate ourselves for it, especially if we can see exactly what buttons the advertisers are pushing, but many of us buy into the images just enough to wish we *could* do it all . . . or could be that thin or that rich or that happy or that confident. And then, telling ourselves that we're not affected by advertising, we find ourselves shelling out for the product.

But we don't buy all the promises or all the images—not to mention all the products—that clamor for us to give them a piece of our minds.

I'm impressed by surveys that tap our reactions to advertising. They keep churning out one dominant complaint: We feel advertising is an insult to our intelligence. Now what exactly does this mean? It means that there's a high incidence of mismatches between how we see ourselves—or would like to see ourselves—and how advertisers portray us. It's as if someone took a picture of you that makes you look dopey and then insisted that you look terrific. It's hard not to feel insulted.

Advertisers don't deliberately insult the people they are trying to seduce; they're basically family-oriented, intelligent, profit-minded sorts who often take really lousy pictures that they think are great shots of their subject. Even more interesting is that we may like how we look in a picture at one point in our lives, and later on feel disgusted or embarrassed by the same photo. What we identified with in an ad five years ago may be completely out of sync with who we are now. And we form these conclusions almost immediately—not from logical deliberation, but by unconsciously weighing all the subtle verbal and nonverbal cues that make up an advertising message. If some of the pieces don't fit, don't ring true—if we don't like how we see ourselves now or how we'd like to see ourselves in the future—we can end up feeling insulted, misunderstood, or confused.

Germaine Monteil introduces
Lift Extrême
Only a face lift makes you feel younger.

Lift Extrême Nutri-Collagen Concentré, supplements the natural development of supportive collagen fibers in your skin to reduce the lined appearance of age. Now your can look as young as you feel.

40 is Fabulous! Are you over 40? Enter The Second Over-40 Beauty Search. Entry forms available at Germaine Monteil counters.

Germaine Monteil's ad for Lift Extrême shows a gorgeous "40 is fabulous" example of how women in this age group might very well wish to look. She's relaxed, wears her white hair proudly, and appears accessible, even attainable, as a role model. But there's a hitch—the copy promises "Only a face lift makes you feel younger."

I conducted in-depth interviews for a skin-care company, and found women were insulted by promises that suggested they were in such bad shape that they needed a face-lift. Mary's reactions to the ad are right to the point: "I look at this and I think, Who are you to tell me how young I feel? You get me thinking about a face-lift, and then I'm not feeling too good. And then I'm thinking maybe *she* had a face-lift and didn't even use your stuff." How is Mary supposed to buy into the image of healthy good looks if she is now ruminating about the prospect of surgery? If a woman is wrinkly enough to consider a face-lift, she's been around long enough to know that little vials of expensive goo aren't about to miraculously take up the slack in her skin. If she's not that wrinkly, the notion of a face-lift simply doesn't relate to her, and she might wonder whether the model had bought her smooth complexion not at Neiman-Marcus but at Plastic Surgery Associates.

The trouble with the advertising mirror is that we never really see ourselves reflected; we only see reflections of what advertisers want us to think their products will do for us. If the image of who we might be if we used the advertiser's product resonates with where we secretly, or not so secretly, wish we were—then there we are, consciously or unconsciously, measuring up to Madison Avenue. Sometimes that's not such a bad thing, but sometimes whatever insecurities we have get exacerbated by advertisers' image-making and by our own intense desires to make it—to win first prize in Madison Avenue's perpetual lookalike contest.

CHAPTER 2

CREATIVE SOLUTIONS THAT AREN'T

Walt is a friend of mine who likes hamburgers a lot. He's a nice-enough guy whose not particularly stylish face is a match for his not even remotely stylish choice of clothing. A computer programmer, his summer casuals consist of white tennis shorts worn with black socks and brown loafers. I've never seen him wear a string tie, but it wouldn't surprise me if his wardrobe matures in that direction.

Now my friend Walt may not be very dapper or socially palatable, but he's a bright, sardonic, witty thinker who's happy to grab a fast-food lunch and work at his desk.

Huge numbers of regular garden-variety people with varying degrees and expressions of nerdiness—with or without the *de rigueur* nerd accessories (white socks/black shoes/spectacles), descend on fast-food restaurants every day. Walt doesn't particularly stand out as uniquely, or even quintessentially, nerdy in these haunts. Sure, put Walt in the corporate offices of, just to grab a wild example, J. Walter Thompson, and he'd look like a nerd's nerd. But at Burger King, he's just some computer programmer buying lunch. In other words, he's just a paying customer. And Burger King wants more customers—a lot more.

So, a while ago now, along comes J. Walter Thompson with a Big Idea for their client, Burger King, a fast-food restaurant with an enormous amount of catching up to do in its perpetual battle against the behemoth that never breaks a sweat, the bane of every other hamburger purveyor out there, the Big Burger in the sky—McDonald's.

J. Walter Thompson's Big Idea is a nationwide search—a contest!—to give a pile of money to the first person to spot the one human in America who's *never* tasted—you guessed it—a Burger King Whopper. The Big Idea that was designed to flood Burger King with ravenous, salivating, paying customers-for-life was *Herb*. In advertising lingo, "Herb" is translated as a "non-user," which means he represents a potential market for Burger King. Goofy? Wait. A goofy concept gets goofier.

Just who is Herb? Herb is Madison Avenue's idea of the Platonic supreme nerd. Herb is Madison Avenue's idea of my friend Walt.

In a damning series of commercials, detailing the pathetic milestones of his life history, we learn that, even to his parents, Herb was "never normal." Called a "nincompoop" by his father and a "little boy" by his mother, Herb is a loser. His friends remember him as "different." Lambasted by his ruler-wielding teacher, who sneers at us, "You had to know how to talk to him," Herb is a loser. The underlying message of the Herb campaign—the psychological pressure point—seems to be: If you don't eat Whoppers, you're a Herb. Pretty persuasive.

Imagine Walt, paying hamburger customer, watching the story

of Herb unfold on his TV screen. Remember, Walt may not be much to look at, but he's no dummy. It's just that Burger King seems to think he is. They didn't *mean* to tell their good old cash-and-carry Walt that they think he's a pitiful jerk. I believe that the advertiser was convinced that it had constructed such a caricature that it couldn't possibly backfire. But the advertiser guessed wrong.

Walt didn't *say* he felt insulted by the Herb commercials; he said they were "stupid." "The Whopper's just a hamburger—who're they kidding? You can get a hamburger anywhere," Walt observed. He's not the only one who was put off. Predictably, Burger King defended the success of the advertising but sales didn't, and the campaign was scrapped after three months. Herb is a creative solution that wasn't.

 On the heels of the debacle that was Herb, Burger King did an abrupt about-face and hurriedly championed homegrown hokiness in its "This is a Burger King town. We know how burgers should be" campaign. And what, you might ask, is a Burger King town? A Burger King town is one that is filled with typical All-American folk—the gorgeous *and* the goofy—eating hamburgers and lavishly licking their fingers. Burger King became no longer a nerd-basher; ordinary, less-than-lovely-looking sorts were held up as the absolutely normal and the absolutely acceptable. A person with nerdy features was no longer dubbed a "nincompoop"; such a creature became the essence of the Burger King town. The soul of America. A valued hamburger customer.

I can easily see my friend Walt tending a backyard barbecue in one of the "This is a Burger King town" spots—complete with his clip-on sunglasses—one of the "real" people (paid actors were shunned) caught on the grainy, shaky footage of a hand-held movie camera. But how much faith could Walt put in Burger King's reformation—in this kind of commercial apologia? Walt wasn't the only guy to wonder, "Is this new stuff supposed to be funny? I don't get it."

How do such sensational gaffes as Herb happen?

Writers and artists who create ads are just people—each has the same kind of unruly primordial unconscious that we all have, each brings quirks and biases and personal histories to creative work. I don't believe that the folks at J. Walter Thompson or at Burger King intended to portray a potential market as objects of derision in ill-fitting suits, but I do believe that an element of unconscious condescension could have helped fuel the flames that embroiled this campaign. After all, it's not altogether inconceivable that people who now win advertising awards for their creative individuality, and even eccentricity, may well have won scorn as oddballs in the past. It's far more ego-gratifying to be an advertising wizard, able to look down on the Herbs and Walts of this world from a superior inside position, than to think the unthinkable: We have seen the mass market, and they are us.

Through the good times and the bad times, J. Walter Thompson, one of the largest, most respected advertising agencies in the world, and Burger King hung in there with each other. Finally, Burger King's sagging sales prompted a new agency search, and the advertiser's huge account was passed to NW Ayer, another fine, well-respected agency, creator of the famous "Be All You Can Be" army campaign.

The news of the demise of J. Walter Thompson's and Burger King's impressive longevity was received in the advertising industry as a truly historical shake-up. For Ayer, the grill got hotter and hotter as their creative solutions to Burger King's slump paraded across American TV screens. The newcomer's innovation? Ayer pounded away on the backyard-grill theme launched by none other than—yes—J. Walter Thompson's "This is a Burger King town" song-and-dance routine. Only *this* time, the new, improved theme line, the one that was supposed to sear its message into Walt's brain and send him sizzling toward the Whopper again, was "We do it like you'd do it, when we do it like we do it at Burger King." Translation: We grill; McDonald's fries. Ours are better than theirs. But Burger King sales continued to slide, and Ayer's been axed.

We've been here before with these two burger battlers. A few years ago, taste tests and contests provided some entertaining commercial moments for the public and some well-needed jolts to

Burger King's bottom line as people chose the "flame-broiled" Burger King over "fried" McDonald's.

It's amusing to have ringside seats at the fights in which grown megabuck companies hurl hamburgers at each other. But once in a while they go too far and the crowd's favorite son gets punched out. Then the fun turns ugly and the crowd gets mad. Such an unfortunate outcome occurred at one of the matches staged during the Battle of the Burgers. J. Walter Thompson had the misguided inspiration to create a spot that put Mr. Rogers in the ring with Burger King. That's Mr. Rogers of Mr. Rogers' Neighborhood, the nicest man on television. Maybe the nicest man in the world. Maybe the nicest man there ever was. This was the man chosen in a rush of creativity to parody in a commercial. A commercial in which a very, very nice man—a Mr. *Rodney*—asks his audience, "Can you say 'McFrying'?" as he accuses McDonald's of inferior hamburger cookery.

In his nicest manner ("He couldn't have been nicer about it," the agency reported), Fred ("Mr.") Rogers explained his concern that it would be harmful for children to see someone they hold as a model of integrity engaged in commercial burger-slinging. Which is to say: Stop airing the spot. Which Burger King did. Quickly. Which was a good thing to do.

The public has principles of taste it doesn't even know about, or think about, until those principles are violated. Then its specific values and beliefs snap into focus, and people attack the desecrators. And often these desecrating pieces of advertising are the by-products of advertisers who chance walking the shaky tightrope between the potential breakthrough of good creative work and the potential breakdown of good taste.

Why did the "Mr. Rodney" topple? Because people get extraordinarily upset when their idols are blasphemed. And Mr. Rogers is a cultural icon of almost mythic proportions among that most zealous lot of Americans, mothers of young children.

Rita is such a parent. She and a small coterie of other young mothers with tots get together every week for a playgroup and watch, among other things, *Mr. Rogers' Neighborhood* with their kids. Rita swears by Mr. Rogers and his wholesomeness so much that she has actually considered banning *Sesame Street* from her children's viewing. Rita tells me: "*Sesame Street* is too glitzy—it's not at all personal. You can trust Mr. Rogers, you know he's giving the kids good values."

My daughter, Julie, is a teenager now, but I remember hearing exactly the same pro-Rogers/anti-*Sesame Street* stance from another mother when our kids were in a playgroup together.

Rita is annoyed when I tell her about the "Mr. Rodney" commercial. She says things like "What are the kids supposed to think? It's like telling them there's no Santa Claus." But she sounds personally affronted, as though her *own* values have been assailed. Rita *believes* in Mr. Rogers. And she's not alone. How could J. Walter Thompson miss it so completely?

The same way the Coca-Cola Company, with its enormous market-research budget, could miss it—and on a fabulously grand scale—when it introduced New Coke to the American public. A phenomenal flop! A screwup the likes of which may have never before been achieved in marketing history! And we were all there.

Somehow, despite all the impressive mounds of data available through the marvels of polls and surveys and focus groups and taste tests, the most critical data of all were never fully tapped: What Coke really *meant* to people—not just how it *tasted*—and how they'd feel if it were *changed.* The arrival of New Coke was followed hotly by the sounds of shoppers scurrying to buy up "old" Coke before it disappeared from their lives forever. New Coke was launched as a *replacement* for what had always been there. The Coke of everyone's childhood was to be expunged, nullified, destroyed.

Unhappy about Pepsi's rubbing Coke's nose in the "Pepsi Challenge" taste tests, which Pepsi invariably won, the Coca-Cola Company went back to the labs and reformulated Coke so that it was sweeter, more like Pepsi, in the hopes that it would come off better in the polls. In fact, Coke's own carefully researched taste tests showed a clear victory for the new formula. But what pleases the palate doesn't necessarily please the heart.

The change turned out to be tantamount to changing the colors of the flag to red, white, and turquoise because turquoise clothing has been selling off the racks for a few seasons. What Coke missed, and missed big, is that the product isn't just a beverage. Coke has been part of Americans' lives for over a hundred years. It's as American as apple pie. It's as American as the flag. Coke *is* America.

When advertisers inadvertently trash basic symbolic values in order to move product—as with Mr. Rogers and Coke—people feel yanked around, misunderstood, and betrayed. But what's amazing is that Coke managed not to know all this. After its initial resolute denials, through grueling soul-searchings, to its final capitulation to public outcry, Coke ended up offering a sincere apology to America and reissued its sacred soda pop as Coca-Cola Classic—a move that resulted in more sales than ever. McCann-Erickson, the agency that developed Coke's advertising through its various incarnations, developed the spot in which the president of Coca-Cola, Don Keogh, soberly told the American public "we have heard you" and announced the decision to bring back the taste of old Coke in the form of Coca-Cola Classic.

How do such colossal blunders happen? By companies paying more attention to their marketing strategies and to the bottom line than to human psychology. By creating advertising that is more in love with itself than in love with the consumer.

In 1984, Chiat/Day created a remarkable commercial for Apple Computer—a spot that ran only once, to the tune of a million dollars, during the Super Bowl, but was a media sensation and triggered an avalanche of successes for Apple. "1984" is a certifiable creative masterpiece; it won the Grand Prix at Cannes and a score of other awards, but what makes it great advertising is that it was in love with *us*, the people it was trying to reach.

"1984" is a sixty-second epic movie in which a vacant-eyed crowd, clothed in Spartan sameness, sits mesmerized before the image of the Orwellian Big Brother on a huge screen. Suddenly, a stunningly powerful female athlete wearing a Macintosh logo runs toward the screen and smashes it to pieces with the force of her sledgehammer. We, the people, are set free. We, the people, bought lots of Apple computers.

Chiat/Day deserved to bask and strut—the agency created a

genuine masterpiece and then—O dreaded opportunity!—they had to do it again. They had to produce another award-winning, sales-soaring masterpiece to run at the 1985 Super Bowl.

Whatever their considerable talent and creative courage, the people at Chiat/Day are subject to the same psychological stresses as the rest of us. And people respond in a variety of ways to serious pressure to reproduce greatness.

What about Chiat/Day's response to pressure? Like the risk-taking agency it is, Chiat/Day met Apple's challenge to reproduce greatness by producing another highly innovative commercial— "Lemmings." But this time, Apple didn't like it. Chiat/Day was supposed to give birth to another wonder child, and it responded to Apple's criticism by insisting that the spot was great anyway.

Some people never even try to hit a winner; somebody else wants it so bad that he'll risk getting thrown out of the game for arguing with the referee. Witness a championship case in point in the person of John McEnroe.

Chiat/Day won its battle with Apple, and "Lemmings" aired exactly one year after "1984." It was a stupendous bomb—the first domino down in a tumble that nearly took Apple off the playing board. "Lemmings" is a fascinating example of a commercial in love with itself. In the spot, blindfolded and briefcased, all wearing the same dark dress-for-success suits, corporate-type men, with a few women sprinkled in, trudge in endless procession, one hand on the shoulder of the next, through a bleak, surreal landscape. Whistling the Seven Dwarfs' hit tune "Heigh-ho, Heigh-ho", but at the pace of a funeral dirge, each of the corporate "lemmings" walks off a rock cliff into the nothingness below. Finally, one stops at the edge, lifts his blindfold, and looks out, as a somber voice warns: "The Macintosh Office. You can look into it or you can go on with business as usual."

"Lemmings" is a frightening, almost macabre spot. The very buyers Apple wanted to attract are sent marching toward certain death, blindfolded by Apple—unwittingly cast as the executioner of its own market. The MBA whiz kid, who finally figures out that he can stop at the edge of the cliff, surreptitiously peeks out. Even he isn't sure he's not going to take the plunge and mindlessly follow the others.

How could people as doltish as these deaf, dumb, and blind

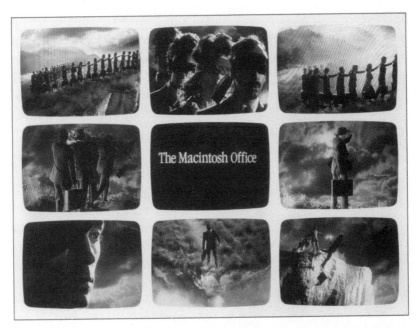

"lemmings" ever learn how to operate The Macintosh Office? There's nothing going on upstairs. The commercial is in love with itself. I believe that Chiat/Day *needed* to be in love with it.

I remember seeing "Lemmings" at a Super Bowl party with a bunch of friends. Granted, we were there as revelers, not researchers, but the spot was greeted with the kind of low moan that could be associated with the sight of a dead animal in the street.

I didn't join the group gasp. I thought it was a wonderful piece of creative work. But then, I like Camus. I just couldn't imagine *The Plague* selling computers. Neither could Brian, the systems analyst of the group. Brian muttered something about whose funeral was it supposed to be, and said, "Yeah. If I don't go buy a Macintosh, I'm going to have to jump off a cliff. You know, come to think of it, I better go warn the department, so they all don't commit suicide tomorrow morning."

The people at Chiat/Day never *intended* to send these messages. They're intelligent, gifted people who no doubt wanted to inspire huge profits for Macintosh. But they loved their commercial so much that they failed to see that the ball they hit was clearly out and risked arguing with the referee—in this case, Apple Computer—and unfortunately for all the players in the game, they won the call.

It's one thing to have a fairly sophisticated business market looking at its peers leaping off a cliff in a surrealistic, metaphorical commercial like "Lemmings," but things start to get even more interesting when an advertiser moves away from symbols into reality to address a young, impressionable market like teenagers. "Lemmings" was a dysphoric fantasy that didn't do much to make its market feel appreciated, but it wouldn't motivate adult businessmen and women to throw themselves off precipices.

But what if you develop a commercial for the teen market—designed to invite their identification—that shows kids driving a  car off a cliff in a high-speed race? This is a new game entirely. It's a game that Hal Riney & Partners and their client, Seattle Pacific, played in creating a spot called "Chickie Race" to sell clothing to teenagers.

"Chickie Race" is shot to look like a scene straight out of James Dean's immortal *Rebel Without a Cause*. A surly hood tough talks a James Dean lookalike at the top of a cliff: "Okay, Johnny-boy, this here's the chickie race. Now, when she gives us the signal, we both go tearing for this here edge, and the first one to bale out of his car is a chicken." The good guy reluctantly agrees. A pony-tailed cheerleader-type signals the start, and the race is on. The bad guy, the challenger, gets his sleeve caught in the gearshift and plunges over the precipice as Johnny-boy rolls away to safety. The horrified teens look over the cliff to see the dead kid's denims floating on the water. And then the tag line appears: "Unionbay. Fashion that's made to last."

I work with teenagers. They do have a weird, sick sense of humor. They can't get enough of the slice-and-dice school of movies. Gary, a senior in a suburban high school, makes honor roll, is the editor of the yearbook, plays varsity basketball, *is nice to his kid sister*, and thinks that *Friday the 13th* is funny. And so do his friends. He tells me they laugh at the parts where Jason hatchets his way into the minds and hearts of his bunk-mates at camp. "It's cool," says Gary with his straight "A"s in English. "I like seeing all the blood and wondering how the next one's gonna get it."

So I believe Ken Mandelbaum, now with Mandelbaum, Mooney & Associates, the writer on the "Chickie Race" spot Hal Riney & Associates created for Seattle Pacific's Unionbay brand clothing, when he tells me what he learned from twenty to thirty focus groups with sixteen-to-twenty-one year old kids. He learned that kids have a weird, sick sense of humor. And that they think most fashion ads are patronizing rip-offs of kids' lives and kids' music. As one whose skin crawls with each commercialization of my beloved Motown, I think so too.

From the advertiser's viewpoint, "Chickie Race" was designed strictly to appeal to kids. If it offended adults, fine—after all, the more Gary's mom hates his music, the better it sounds to him. Seattle Pacific's Unionbay clothing line is a pebble in the midst of mountains like Jordache and Calvin Klein and Levi's. Seattle Pacific saw "Chickie Race" and had to have it—had to get its brand name out fast. And it was already clear to Hal Riney that the client needed something "edgy" to defeat the looming bogeyman of clutter—to get the maximum impact out of Unionbay's $2 million ad budget.

With "Chickie Race," Unionbay's name did get out there. But not for long. The spot was test-marketed only in Los Angeles and was picked up by the likes of *CBS Evening News*, in its coverage of hot new advertising, around the same time the retailers started getting irate calls from adults. Two weeks later, the spot was pulled. Viewers were scared and angry. Scared that kids would go out and copy the commercial and get killed playing chicken. Angry that tragedy was treated so tastelessly and with such detachment.

As a writer wanting to see his work accomplish what it was designed to do, Ken Mandelbaum wishes that the spot got a chance to air nationally—that the Unionbay brand had had a chance to be embossed on the public's mind alongside of Levi Strauss & Company. From a *marketing* perspective, he's probably right. Unionbay would definitely have made more of a name for itself. And I don't doubt his being right about kids finding the spot a real hoot—kids do revel in perverse humor. But he and his were so focused on the bottom line that they forgot all about who pays the clothing bills.

From a marketing perspective, for advertising to be a productive sales hook, it has to get the people with the money on its side.

"Chickie Race" went after exactly the right market, used its native language, and even alienated the right people—parents—to ingratiate itself with teenagers. But the adults who put the commercial together and the adults who fell in love with what the spot could do to get the brand name in lights and set sales on fire identified so much with the kids' perspective that they cut off the purse strings. A spot may have a narrow target, but TV doesn't permit an exclusive audience. The advertiser forgot who pays the bills. Creative? Yes. Solution? No.

What about the adult audience whose protests about "Chickie Race" so quickly terminated its TV life? Unlike the advertiser, *they* didn't *want* the spot to work. They were scared of copycats. Do kids really mimic what they see in the media?

Common sense says yes. We've all read grim news stories about teen-pact suicides that were followed in rapid succession by others across communities and across the country. Or about a kid who defends his extreme violence in committing a murder with, as I recently read, "I just seen it on TV."

Social learning theory says yes. Children learn about social behavior by imitating others. Albert Bandura, Ph.D., an outstanding research psychologist, conducted controlled experiments that showed that kids imitated the behavior of others who were shown to them on videotapes just as much as if they were "real."

Clinical experience says yes. I've worked with kids in mental hospitals who've *told* me about the movies and stories that affected them, that went into the mix of their own frustrations and anger and insecurities and helped point a path to their own destruction. Cynthia comes to mind. I met her when she was sixteen. She had just got her license and had just got drunk and wrecked her parent's car speeding around a curve into a tree. Miraculously, she emerged physically intact, but feeling suicidal. I wanted to get to know her.

> "I've been drinking beer since I was fourteen," Cynthia tells me with a flip of her long black hair. "My parents were always too dumb to notice. I can handle it—I don't usually get drunk. I guess I'm just a party animal," she says with a half-laugh, half-hitch in her voice.
>
> "Right. And you've just had the time of your life."
>
> Cynthia sends me an icy stare. "Look, I'm sick

of jerk doctors and my parents' bullshit. I'd love
to make them suffer."

"Do they drink?"

"Only at 'Happy Hour' as my mother calls it.
Which for her is any hour she wants. And *never*
beer. That's *my* drink."

"Okay, why's that *your* drink?"

"I like it, that's all," she shoots back. "I just
like action."

"And beer means action?"

"Yeah"—Cynthia smirks—"unless you're an
old bag like my *mother*."

"What happened last week when you got drunk?"

"I don't know, it just kind of happened. But I
was really mad at my parents. They promised to
get me a car and then they said they wouldn't until
my *grades* got better. But they're always too busy
to help me. They just yell at me to go do my homework. I don't like them and they don't like me."

"And you don't like yourself much either."

"Drop dead," Cynthia says to me, but her glare
has softened.

Certainly, Cynthia's beer drinking wasn't *caused* by advertising—that problem was only a symptom of deeper problems—
but images of frothy fun and frolic helped reinforce a direction of
escape that almost did her in. In a later session, she laughingly
asked me if I thought she could ever be as happy as the "Beer
Bunnies," as she derisively called them, looked on television. She
meant the question to be rhetorical, but her bitterness about the
illusion was obvious.

What if an ad is in good taste, but the stuff being sold is
deadly—like cigarettes? The tobacco industry deals with the moral
issue of selling a deadly product by transforming it into a marketing
issue. It argues that advertising can only prompt a change in brand
usage. The cigarette companies claim their ads can't possibly turn
a nonsmoker into a smoker.

Research can judge the cigarette companies right, or judge them
wrong, depending on who conducts the survey. The Tobacco Institute *still* maintains that there is no proven link between lung
cancer and cigarette smoking. And furthermore, the companies
maintain that despite the fresh faces in their advertising, they in
no way *intend* for young people to *start* smoking.

In the meantime, young women comprise America's fastest-growing population of smokers. In the meantime, we see a company like R. J. Reynolds advertising its Camel cigarettes with a campaign, created by McCann-Erickson, that features friendly cartoon camels having a great time and that invites people of a certain cartoon-loving age to "Party with the Wild Pack." In a truly awe-inspiring display of poor taste, a recent magazine insert for the "Joe Camel" campaign details a method for impressing women at the beach: "Run into the water, grab someone and drag her back to the shore as if you've saved her from drowning. The more she kicks and screams, the better." Boys will be boys. Feed a rape fantasy, sell a cigarette. In the wake of "Joe Camel," R. J. Reynolds fired McCann-Erickson.

Actually, one of the more bizarre ad campaigns around, created by BBDO, Pepsi's agency, for Kent cigarettes, wouldn't have started anyone smoking. It just might have qualified as one of the best *antismoking* ads ever to run in recent years. Directly under the Surgeon General's warning: "Quitting Smoking Now Greatly Reduces Serious Risks to Your Health," the ad has the headline "The experience you seek. Kent." What *is* that experience? Death. What's

missing? Life. The shadows, the
ghosts of a couple looking into the
beyond, as cold, snow-covered
hills rise around them, dominate
the picture. The male ghost holds
a cigarette. The creative unconscious was working overtime on
this one.

Being a smoker in America is
distinctly losing points in the win-
ning-friends-and-influencing-
people department. Everywhere
smokers turn, they are faced with
stomach-churning medical coun-
sel, dramatic spasms of hacking,
disdainful glowerings, and unsolicited advice on quitting. When
I'm with a smoker who answers, "Smoking, please," to the host-
ess's seating question, the scene always reminds me of the one in
Monty Python's *Life of Brian*, where, on Good Friday, prisoners
are directed toward the proper sentencing: "Crucifixion? Right
this way."

Even the most powerful selfdefenders *have* to fight off the
nagging chill lurking in the comforting curls of smoke: This just
might kill me. The last thing a smoker needs, if the advertiser wants
him to keep on puffing (and it just might; the sixteen-to-twenty-
one-year-olds are puffing more than ever) is to be graphically reminded of the consequences of not heeding the Surgeon General's
warning. In this ad, Kent is unconsciously telling its consumer
market that it's suicidal.

How could such a blatantly off-base ad get produced? Couldn't
some bright writer, or product manager, or account executive, or
secretary, have turned green with the sinking intuition that something was dreadfully wrong here? Maybe somebody turned green,
but the show went on anyway. And it probably went on because,
to the collective unconscious of the people behind the campaign,
the link of death with smoking is true—and the truth tends to
leak out.

Kent's public-relations department reported that there was essentially nothing wrong with the campaign; the advertiser simply

Kent.
The choice is taste.

SURGEON GENERAL'S WARNING: Cigarette
Smoke Contains Carbon Monoxide.

The low-tar family with taste.

decided to change creative strategies. At the same time, the ad industry's Holy Scriptures—*Adverising Age* and *Adweek*—crackled with negative commentaries on the campaign, most of which could be summarized as "I'm glad *I* didn't write that." Still maintaining it had made no error in judgment, Kent whipped up another ad to take the place of its CigaSuicide campaign. This one is all light and bright colors. Ah, spring! That's what smoking's all about! Gone are the dark, shadowy figures (gone are the implications of dark, shadowy spots on lungs).

Sometimes a highly creative campaign is successful and on target, but contains one clunker. With Kent, the whole series was a fiasco. With the campaign Doe-Anderson created for St. Anthony Hospital in Louisville, one ad got flak in an otherwise effective creative solution to the advertiser's problems.

Given the intensity of the competition in Humana Hospital-dominated Louisville, it was imperative that 374-bed St. Anthony carve out a distinct and memorable personality for itself. What Doe-Anderson did with its campaign, particularly with the "St. Anthony as a St. Bernard" piece, is to transform a hospital building into a living being. The ad brings a saint to life. Which is, in itself, a masterful message about the healing powers of a medical institution. In "St. Bernard," a cold marble statue becomes a living, panting image of man's best friend—and a "lifesaver" at that. Not a bad metaphor at all. Very creative.

The clunker is also very creative. Kindly Sister Alwinia is pictured beneath the boldfaced headline "She wants to have your baby." Yikes. I showed this ad to Mary, who happens to be Roman Catholic. She's pregnant with her first child. Thirty years old, Mary is the product of a parochial-school education, complete with ruler-happy nuns. She *tried* to be a good girl—she tried so hard that all her emotions are still neatly knotted and bundled today.

St. Anthony as a St. Bernard.

In the Alps, the big, shaggy St. Bernard is viewed as a lifesaver, because he braves the elements in search of those who are hurt or lost.

Well, there's a little of the St. Bernard in our own mission here at St. Anthony Hospital.

You see, we recognize that our responsibilities don't stop at the boundaries of the hospital grounds.

That's why we've established outreach programs like "Contact" that go out into the community to provide assistance to those who have trouble caring for themselves.

We've also taken our "Feeling Good" program into the schools to try and help children understand the value and responsibility of good health.

In fact, much like the St. Bernard, we'll go wherever and do whatever we can to help. It's not the traditional role for a hospital, but it may be one of the most vital services any hospital can provide to the community.

St. Anthony Hospital

Mary literally blanched when she saw the Sister Alwinia ad. When she was a kid, she tells me, she felt the nuns wanted to control her every thought, to destroy her identity. "There's something scary about this ad. It must bring back all those times in school when I thought Sister Anna hated me. She used to tell me that I was a good girl now, but my long blond hair was going to get me in trouble someday. That I should cut it short. That I was too pretty for my own good. She always made me feel guilty and frightened. It's strange but this ad scares me. I know that doesn't make sense."

St. Anthony is open to all people, but it *is* a Catholic Hospital. Mary is Roman Catholic, but you don't have to be Roman Catholic to be unnerved—if only on an unconscious level—by the image of a childless elderly woman grasping for the baby she can never have. This is the stuff that gets passed through the culture in myths and fairy tales. Now, as anyone who's ever read the unhomogenized versions of fairy tales knows, they tend to be filled with unsavory occurrences such as carnage and cannibalism, kidnapping and abandonment, lust and greed.

Sister Alwinia has the kindest, sweetest face you ever saw, but "she wants to have your baby." The unconscious is always on the lookout—beware, looks can be deceiving. Mary's blanching when she saw the ad was instantaneous. She didn't have to stop and analyze the message to react. Neither did the people who called St. Anthony to complain about the ad;

She wants to have your baby.

Sister Alwinia has never had children of her own. And yet, more than 55,000 babies have started their lives with the warmth of Sister's care.

Along the way, she's touched the lives, not only of these newborns, but of their parents as well with some notable Louisville firsts.

It was Sister Alwinia's concern for the family that first allowed fathers in the delivery room to share the experience of their baby's birth.

It was Sister, too, who began "rooming in," helping mother and child share this important time together.

And it was Sister Alwinia who first allowed children to visit their new brothers or sisters at the hospital.

So if you want your baby to be born in a warm, supportive, family-oriented environment, remember St. Anthony's Family Unit and Sister Alwinia. She wants to have your baby.

they knew they were somehow offended. To some, I suspect, the subtle sacrilege of a nun offering herself as a surrogate was emotionally disruptive. To some, it may even have been offensive in its implicit demand for a woman to give up her unwanted baby to the good sister rather than have an abortion.

Did the agency realize the ad could resonate with such negative unconscious associations? Yes and no. Did St. Anthony Hospital realize that the ad could boil up a cauldron of emotions? Yes and no. Yes, they knew it was controversial. Yes, they knew it was an attention-grabber. No, the depths of these psychological reactions weren't part of their strategic planning. But they knew they had to fill beds, and they wanted to take creative risks.

What about Sister Alwinia? She really exists, and she really is a wonderful lady. When Doe-Anderson's client saw the sketch for the "She Wants to Have Your Baby" ad, they didn't know what to do. So they decided to show it to Sister Alwinia herself, a ninety-two-year-old nearly blind nun. If she approved it, even in its rough form, then the ad would be acceptable. The client thought the ad would be as dead as a doornail. Jay Giles, the agency's creative director, who was there, told me what happened:

"She held it right up to her face—and there was a long, long, long wait. Finally, someone asked, 'What do you think, Sister?' 'Oh, I don't know,' she finally said. 'Do you think I can have fifty copies for my relatives in Germany?' "

A lot of hearts were in the right place in developing this ad, it's just that the unconscious can't always be counted on to be so benign in its interpretations. St. Anthony Hospital got some warm letters about Sister Alwinia and a saintly patina rubbed off on its image in Louisville, but it doesn't change the disturbing underpinnings of the ad.

At times then, advertisers and their agencies can concoct startlingly creative solutions that fail to connect with consumers because they haven't taken into account the psychological complexities of the people they are selling to. Sometimes, as with "Lemmings," advertisers are just too stuck in the world they created. Sometimes, as with Coke, they mistake the fantastic stage sets they design for reality itself. With these kinds of mix-ups, no wonder ads sometimes come across as having confused personalities, and send contradictory messages. And no wonder advertisers don't always know about them.

CHAPTER 3

CONTRADICTIONS ADVERTISERS DON'T KNOW ABOUT

She walks coolly into my office, a tall woman, more handsome than pretty, in a perfectly tailored Chanel suit, carrying her polished leather briefcase with an easy air. Her short, neat, light brown hair is clipped to reveal small pearl earrings. Samantha is an extremely successful attorney. By all reports, she is brilliant. I ask her why she is interested in therapy at this point in her life. As soon as she opens her mouth to speak, I sense the answer.

At thirty-seven, this model of intellectual acumen and aplomb has the voice of a little girl. A very little girl. Startlingly squeaky and nasal, Samantha tells me her concern: "I know exactly where I want to go with this firm and I know exactly how to get there. I know I'm considered a star player—my work is impeccable. But I'm running into a resistance I don't understand, and I don't like that feeling. I like to be in control, and there's something that doesn't add up here."

Samantha is right. Something doesn't add up, and that something is the match between her voice and the rest of what she presents as herself. And people pick up on these inconsistencies with incredible speed. Samantha's colleagues may not even be able to admit or clearly identify what they're reacting to in her, but regardless of her expertise and composure in the toughest situations, regardless of her contributions to the firm, they can't quite envision her as a partner.

All of us get confused, annoyed, bored, or distrustful of people who have inconsistencies in their personalities. The same thing happens with ads that are filled with contradictory messages. We feel comfortable with people who say what they mean, and sound the way they look, and present a picture of one person rather than fragments of several. We may not like them, but at least we have a sense of who they are and what we can expect of them.

When there's a glaring gap between how an ad looks and what it says, or how it says it, it can come across as if it has some kind of personality disorder. We don't warm up to people—or to ads —who send mixed messages.

Early on in my work, I was asked by one of my clients, a huge manufacturer of "personal products" like toothpaste, deodorant, and shampoo, to analyze a creative concept its agency had developed to promote a new shampoo. My client was no different from many others—he was worried.

My client was worried because an alarmingly high percentage of new products fail—about 80 percent—and he was the product manager. So he wanted to stack the cards as much as he could on the side of winning a very difficult, high-stakes game, the game of introducing yet another shampoo to American women already awash in a sea of hair-soap options all claiming to perform the same miracles. His company's miracle? *This* shampoo made an exceptionally abundant amount of lather.

Worry is why my client asked me to study a storyboard—

sketches and copy, laid out in a cartoon-frame succession, that capture the main points and actions of a proposed TV commercial. The agency assured the product manager that the board would make a great spot, but my client wanted to make sure he wasn't missing something, even something subtle, that could undermine the message. After all, he's been around, and is no stranger to the fact that what he's got to sell, in thirty glorious seconds or less, is basically just another parity shampoo.

When I analyzed the storyboard, I saw some inherent contradictions that could spell confusion at best and rejection at worst. Now, the world of advertising does not operate in time as we know it. Its world is a perpetual state of fast-forward/fast-reverse/hypertime where "on time" does not exist. Almost without exception, all projects must be "done yesterday," or nameless, but nonetheless catastrophic, consequences will ensue. In this case, the usual time machine was fully operational, and in light of the deadline for the product launch, I needed to present my analysis to my client *and* the agency in an urgent, next-day meeting.

The problems in the storyboard boiled down to a case of mistaken identity, brought on by conflicting information. The confusion could be cleared up fairly easily, but that happy conclusion wasn't even heard by the agency until we'd gone through a familiar communications dance.

I pointed out that the storyboard's picture of a woman washing her hair in a bathtub, surrounded by lather, looked more as if it were selling bubble bath than even a super-duper sudsing shampoo. Furthermore, I noted, women don't wash their hair while taking a bath. This may seem straightforward, but then the dance steps get somewhat complicated. "Look, you're getting too deep into this," the art director snapped at me with a wave of his hand. "I *meant* for there to be so much lather that it would feel like pampering—that's why she's taking a bath." I explained that, unless the marketing strategy included persuading consumers that they can take a bubble bath as well as wash their hair with this particular shampoo, the product suffered from a split personality.

"Besides," argued the writer, "I thought having her wash her hair in the bath was sensual and different; it doesn't look like all the other shampoo-in-the-shower commercials." True. But what about reality? I invited him and the rest of the small group of men constituting our meeting—writer, artist, research director, product manager, account supervisor—to think of any woman they'd ever seen who washed her hair while taking a bath. They couldn't. But why all the fuss? Why the defensive display? Why the dance?

People generally dislike admitting they're wrong, that they've missed something. Especially something obvious. And in the frenzy of artificial, desperate deadlines, agencies often feel they can't afford to go back to the drawing board. In this instance, my client was enormously helpful. Not only did he agree with my analysis (and what could be more helpful to a consultant than that?) but he stepped into *real* time and pushed back the production date. A rare bird. At that point, the agency could afford to see the problems with the bath execution, and developed a creative strategy more in keeping with how women actually use shampoo. The epilogue? To this day, despite all the frantic deadlines, the product *still* hasn't been launched.

Get your music in shape.

Often ads with internal contradictions, with personality conflicts, *do* get produced, and are sent out to try to sell products anyway. This ad never even had a chance. It was conceived in a cross-cultural fantasyland and delivered by a myriad of butter-fingered midwives. The advertising manager for JVC Company of America's High Fidelity Division took whatever heroic measures he could at the time of this ad's development, to ease its way into print, but the deck was already stacked against him.

It seems that most of JVC's creative direction came from the parent company in Japan, and that the hot item on *its* worldwide advertising program was aerobics. What this meant was that Japan wanted to use the same aerobics ad theme and design for *all* of JVC's international divisions, regardless of cultural interpretation. Regardless of target market.

And that's not all. The ad manager didn't just receive creative suggestions from Japan, he received the *photo* to be used in this ad. That's what Marstellar, the agency on the piece, had to work with in order to hook male consumers, the heaviest purchasers of stereo equipment.

I wish I could say something empathetic and positive about the ad that emerged from all of this, but I can't. It suffers from a glaring case of contradictory copy and visuals.

Visually, the ad is dominated by a graceful, static young woman wearing a white leotard and a vacuous expression. She is seated on the pale carpet of a balanced, monochromatic room. The mood is serene. It would be natural to associate quiet background music with this theme, perhaps something reminiscent of swans on a lake.

The copy opener tells us that if we "want quiet background music, there are plenty of systems to choose from." I have to assume that this refers to systems *other* than the advertiser's.

The next line claims that if we are "the high-energy type who likes music the same way," we'd go for the JVC system. Since it is reasonably safe to assume that the advertiser wouldn't deliberately highlight the benefits of its "quiet background music" competitors, I can only conclude that the photo is intended to portray a "high-energy type."

The tag line below the Slender Seated Female exhorts, "Get your music in shape." It takes a lofty *grand jeté* indeed to leap from a shapely body to shapely music. Even if we land on our feet in a perfect fourth position, what have we learned about JVC's benefits as a sound system? Then there's the implicit assumption that quiet background music is somehow unshapely, or even flabby. What does this say about folks reading this ad who actually *like* quiet background music?

If this ad is targeted to high-energy types who wouldn't be caught dead with quiet background music wafting through their living rooms, this ad's in trouble.

What is needed is some cohesion between the copy and the visuals, as there needs to be cohesion between Samantha's appearance and her voice. What is needed is an accurate, believable representation of the consumer in his or her natural habitat, doing high-energy things. Psychologically, it makes no sense to talk about high-energy people and high-energy music in a world of soft white, off-white, and gray.

High-energy means high-intensity color and motion. If JVC chose to stand behind the position of creating shapely music (for reasons I can't fathom), it would have alleviated at least some of this ad's emotional stress if the "shapes" of its visuals and copy matched.

Companies may end up accepting creative solutions that they feel uneasy about but don't exactly know why. Perhaps that's what happened with this ad for JVC. For my part, I felt sorry for the ad manager. He was stuck. But he didn't really see the contradictions. He was just following orders.

If a person's verbal language doesn't match her body language, we can't figure out where her real communication is coming from, let alone decide whether or not we want to play ball with him. Seagram's Seven Crown served up a confused, conflict-ridden ad several years ago, created by Ogilvy & Mather (founded by the great David Ogilvy of *Confessions of an Advertising Man*), that implicitly tells us "Come hither" and "Get lost"—at the same time. All it *thinks* it's saying is "Let's party."

Boldly upright and flanked by burly, tumbler-sized glasses of liquor stands the product, underlined by the pronouncement "Seagram's Seven gets things stirring." Receding into the back corner are the presumed participants in all this excitement, done up in color and lighting reminiscent of neon painting on black velvet.

Seagram's Seven gets things stirring.

The people proving Seagram's success at "stirring" aren't really laughing; their eyes stay model wide and their mouths and bodies are held in the stiffly tilted postures of store mannequins that are supposed to demonstrate riotous good times.

There's a huge gap between how the Seagram's ad *looks* and what it *says*. While the come-hither singles-bar girls are busily aiming their animated versions of sexuality at the dashing eligible male in the scene, the staid, staunchly unmoving, immovable Seagram's bottle and glasses dominate the page, barricading us from all that fun like a kind of paternalistic road block to the promised pleasure.

As part of a project in which I analyzed the "personalities" of different ads for musk colognes, Jacqueline Cochran, Inc., asked me to study an ad for Chaps Musk by Ralph Lauren. It suffers from a type of personality ambivalence similar to Seagram's.

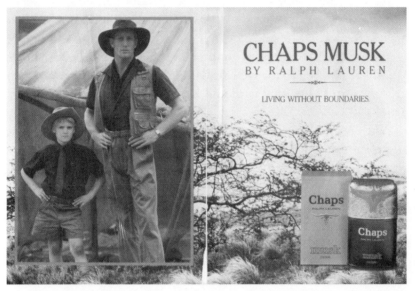

Shot in sepia tones, the backdrop of the Chaps Musk ad, developed by Cosmair, Inc., sets the stage for a rough, wide-open safari fantasy. But while the background music hums "Don't Fence Me In," and the marquee boasts the picture's title "Living Without Boundaries," our heroes are saying something very different, and all without uttering a word. There they are, man and boy, living solidly *within* the boundaries of their own personal borders.

Set apart from the natural environment, safely packaged in their gray rectangle, the protagonists don't look as though they're having much fun out there on the range. The man's expression is flat. The boy presses his lips into a slight scowl. With their defiant arms-on-hips stance, they defend their own personal fences against invasion by the outside world. Even the relationship between them is cold, rigidly bounded rather than being opened up by the freedom implied by "Living Without Boundaries."

How could Chaps Musk end up with such a mixed-up identity?

I believe its personality problems stem from its Ralph Lauren designer-clothing roots. It has always appeared to me that the Ralph Lauren "look" is one of carefully constructed informality, that the men who are attracted to it are probably city-bound folks with little hope of leading an outdoor life. The *illusion* of being more rugged, casual, and free than they really are is a powerful draw. Like the guys in the Chaps Musk ad, they *wish* they could live "without boundaries." After all, even if Ralph Lauren is trying to reach the boy within the man who yearns to live in the wide-open spaces, the kid in the ad is wearing a necktie like a good little lad, even when he's hanging around his tent. The fantasy of Chaps Musk is reassuring to the well-dressed, fashion-conscious man who still dreams of chucking it all and heading for the hills like Albert Brooks in *Lost in America*.

With Kathy Keeton, vice-chairman of General Media, president of Penthouse International's *Longevity Magazine*, things were a bit different. She *meant* to use a mixed message to introduce the publication to media buyers, a group she describes as a "sophisticated advertising audience inundated by clutter." The ad, developed in-house, ran in *Advertising Age* and drew 250 calls from media buyers. I'd say it broke through their clutter all right.

"She's 70," the headline boldly asserts beneath the smiling photo of the young woman in her late thirties hoisting free weights. A variety of interpretations come to mind in an effort to make sense out of this contradiction. The woman is a magna-cum-laude graduate of cosmetic surgery. She is an android. She is Goldie Hawn in her younger days suppressing a paroxysm of giggles at the public's gullibility. *Longevity* actually imagined that its media buyers would not only buy space in the magazine, but buy the idea that this gal could possibly *be* seventy and buy the magazine's promise of a "voyage toward immortality" (as the ad's copy boasts). But in the canniest of ploys, and in the tiniest of type, the "truth" appears in the lower right-hand corner of the ad—*upside down:* "Featured profile is a dramatization."

Kathy Keeton wanted to milk the greatest possible "suspense" out of the mismatch between the message of the headlines and the message in the picture. But *Longevity* is a health magazine targeted to the elderly. A sizable group of advertisers are creating ads that suggest they are finally paying attention to the studies that have consistently appeared in all the major advertising-research journals in recent years that characterize older Americans as smart, skeptical, sexy, and lively—and with plenty of money to spend in the advertiser's store that treats them right. Even though the ad was not designed to pitch *Longevity* to consumers, young media buyers aren't the only readers of *Advertising Age*, and the ad communicates a perception of its consumer market that once again choruses America's old cultural anthem: Youth at all costs!

SHE'S 70.

INTRODUCING LONGEVITY MAGAZINE!

LONGEVITY

I keep my mouth shut and show the ad to my mother.

Jessie is sixty-eight years old, has the body of a wood sprite, plays the drums in a community band, travels all over the world with my father, Ralph (a human hydroplane himself), and speaks her mind. "How could they put that face there? It's so wrong I don't believe it. Even with a face-lift she wouldn't look like that —she'd have to have some maturity. Seventy is real. Longevity is real. This is so false it's ridiculous! To me it's very dishonest. There's plenty of false advertising—I've been disillusioned many times. It's like a joke. It's like telling me I don't know what I look like. Well, I know what I look like."

Jessie's not the only spry gray-boomer who would take exception to *Longevity*'s manner of baiting the hook for its media buyers. Erin is sixty-five years old, dresses well, is attractive— wrinkles and all—and looks just about her age. She started therapy to try to put her life together after her husband's accidental death a year ago. "At least I'm old enough to think for myself," Erin remarked at one point. "Everywhere you look, all the ads say you have to be young—you have to be gorgeous. That stuff doesn't get to me anymore like it used to. I don't have to look like Joan Collins. She's a phony anyway, just like the rest of those Hollywood hacks."

Besides "immortality," *Longevity*'s ad promises that the magazine will "cut through the clutter and confusion and separate myth from medical reality." Tell that to Jessie! Sell that to Erin! Bedazzled by their own cleverness, the folks at *Longevity* went ahead and offered a myth that successfully reeled in the narrow media-buyer market they were after, but presented an insulting image of the very consumers they hoped would actually buy the subscriptions.

Longevity's ad rhapsodizes in its body copy that it is an "upscale health and science publication" that will tell its market, dullards with dough, "What to eat, when to eat, where to live, who to trust." I could just imagine Maggie Kuhn, vociferous leader of the Gray Panthers, sinking her choppers into *that* pile of patronization—so I sent her the ad and called her. Here's what she had to say:

> The picture is unreal. It just reinforces the classic myth that youth is great and old age is a disaster. It affirms the belief that old age is a time to play— like the copy says—to play tennis and eat the right food and who to trust. Old age is a time to reflect—to use your own sense of history, to respond in a positive way to change. Not that play couldn't be a part of it, but if all you do is play— what a waste!

> The elders of the tribe should be concerned not about *their* survival, but about the survival of the tribe. This ad is a trivialization of age and its experience with change and its historical perspective. I find it revolting. *Longevity*'s philosophy denies the continuity of life and the universal experience of aging that has enabled the human species to survive by *coping* with change.

> Just having a young face and working hard at it is not really a basis for sturdy self-esteem. Self-esteem is built on mind and spirit—reinforced by having a purpose for your life, a goal of working with others to make our troubled, competitive society a just and peaceful society.

> George Bernard Shaw once observed that wrinkles
> are credentials of our humanity. The cosmetic im-
> age of a young face is not reality.

Like *Longevity,* one of the ads in a series developed a few years
ago by William Esty Company for Tambrands, uses a contradictory visual message. Unlike *Longevity,* it didn't mean to. In the
process, Tambrands' point self-destructs by unintentionally un-
dermining the very message it tries to send.

Let's start at the beginning. Tambrands wanted the teenage
market. It wanted girls to identify with, and recognize themselves
in, the Tampax ads the advertiser developed in order to communicate with them. According to Mark Miller, who was, at the time,
the management supervisor at Esty, the creative strategy was for
"real life to be the unifying factor" throughout the series, which
was to be based on the premise, gleaned from the true confessions
of consumer research, that girls start out using sanitary pads, but
switch to tampons when they get older.

The mother-and-daughter ad in the series Esty created to persuade girls to go ahead and make the switch to tampons presents
a unified front. It's a wonderful image—the kindly mom, the warm
daughterly embrace, the open discussion about menstruation products. But market research and clinical experience suggest that many
teens feel they can't really talk to their mothers about intimate

THE TAMPAX SERIES. AD.NO.6

**Did you think Mom wanted
you to use pads forever?**

Do you remember the first time you had this talk with Mom? Well we
understand that Mom would first tell you to use pads. That's because her
Mother probably told her the same thing. But like most Moms, she didn't
mean that to be forever. So, if you're still using pads maybe you should
reconsider why Tampax tampons might be better.

Tampax is internal protection, so you'll feel cleaner, cleaner than you
would with any pad. And feeling cleaner is more comfortable. There's no
bulk, no mess, no odor. It can actually change the way you
feel about your period.

And here's one other nice reason to switch—
Tampax has had over 45 years of experience
with tampons. More than anyone else.
Maybe that's why more women use Tampax
than any other tampon or pad.   **TAMPAX. FEELING CLEANER CAN CHANGE THE
WAY YOU FEEL ABOUT YOUR PERIOD.**

subjects like this, and look outside for straight talk. No matter, this "real-life vignette" is a fantasy with which girls *wish* they could identify, and Tambrands set itself up as a kind of mother-substitute to answer their questions.

The mother-daughter ad isn't actually suggesting that girls check out the answer with their mothers when it asks, "Did you think Mom wanted you to use pads forever?" By portraying a secure, loving bond, Tambrands is giving proxy permission to teens to go out and buy Tampax, saying implicitly, "Don't worry, you're not doing anything your mother wouldn't approve of—you're still a good girl." The visuals are integrated with the copy and with the psychological facts of life for teenage girls.

"At 13, I used pads."   "At 19, I switched to Tampax tampons. One definitely feels cleaner."

Not so with the split-face ad in the same series. Here, double messages collide, and any resemblance to "real life" is strictly coincidental. The problem lies in the obvious use of a *single* face, of a *single* age to symbolize a "real" passage from the early to late teen years. In the rather bizarre photo, one side of the model's face poses as herself at a younger age: "At 13, I used pads," *this* side tells teenagers. The other side of the face, made up and coiffed to cue an older image, declares, "At 19, I switched to Tampax tampons. One definitely feels cleaner."

Apart from the ancient equation of menstruation with filth and contamination—an archaic view at best—the sheer bizarreness of the visual image is off-putting in its own right. How is a teenage girl supposed to feel respected as a reasonable person when six years of living are represented by nothing more than the superficial addition of cosmetic decoration? True, kids like to look older, and they like to slap on makeup to convince others of their advanced age, but Tambrands intended to portray the kind of maturity its market needs to decide on its own to buy tampons. The advertiser missed the mark when it linked growing up with dressing up rather than with the inner confidence and independence that evolves with experience and with the *real* passage of time. Tambrands missed the mark here because it fails to take the position of an empathetic adult—the position it did take in the mother-daughter ad.

In the split-face ad, the advertiser is just another teenage girl with a false ID trying to pass. The ad is attention-grabbing all right, but taking a chance on getting carded and losing credibility is risky business for an advertiser. The people who designed this ad meant to do exactly the opposite, but they unintentionally told teens that they really don't take them seriously.

The point is that subtle confusions in ads can turn people off at a gut level without their knowing why, and advertisers just go on naively churning out work that is sometimes literally nauseating when it's meant to be appetizing. For example, take a look at the ad created by Isidore & Paulson for Midori Melon Liqueur, a product of Suntory International.

Midori wants us to "MIXA-BATCHOFMELONBALLS" (translation: make a punch with its melon liqueur). Midori wants us to mix up so much punch that we'd have to use a goldfish bowl. It even offers to send us a free recipe book.

Now who sends for recipes? Women. What woman in her right mind would, as the copy in-structs, "Tell the goldfish to move over," empty out the goldfish bowl, stick the occupants into a curiously unmarked measuring cup, and—*voilà!*—fill up the goldfish residence with algae-colored liquid to serve her guests? Not Marilyn, that's for sure.

Marilyn gives lots of pool parties and serves lots of spiked punch. Her house is very tidy and very clean. I showed her the ad. "There's something revolting about the way the punch looks," Marilyn says to me with a face that looks like she's just spotted a cockroach in her kitchen. "It's not very appetizing. And what are the fish supposed to be doing?"

Marilyn doesn't have to go through a thinking process to *react* to the ad; she never has to consciously put together the relationship between fish droppings, algae, and appetite loss. But it's all there, and it happens very fast. And all the advertiser is trying to do is "be creative." But the messages don't add up.

As nutty as Midori's ad for a truly unique punch is, it pales beside Westwood One's ad for its radio-network services. Picture this: You're a media manager for an ad agency, and your job is to place radio spots so that they pull in the "right target listener." You're flipping through *Advertising Age* and you stop at a full-color, full-page ad filled by a photo taken from the back of a little boy taking a leak in the toilet. The headline reads "The success of target advertising, like so many things in life, is ultimately a matter of aim." Does it catch your attention? You bet. Is it kind of cute? You bet. But who's the kid supposed to be? The guy who's got to carefully "aim" his radio spot at the right target is the media manager. Okay, so it's the media-manager-as-pissant. And what's he aiming for? The audience, of course. So, it's the public-as-toilet.

These image translations didn't make this ad, created in-house, any less amusing to its media-manager market—nor should they. The whole point, according to Mark Specter, national director of advertising and creative for Westwood One, was to create an ad that would attract attention and stand out from the clutter—just like with the *Longevity* piece. "It's common in Europe and Japan to use this style of advertising—and particularly to use kids," Mr. Specter explained. And it did get noticed!

In today's teeming marketplace, getting noticed is the *modus operandi* of advertisers. And it needs to be. If an ad doesn't grab attention, it's dead in the water. But getting noticed doesn't necessarily correlate with being persuasive or effective any more than it does when a class clown tries desperately not to be ignored. Grabbing attention at any cost can backfire even more expensively. Just because you remember somebody's face doesn't mean you'd like him or trust him enough to bring him home to dinner. Or buy stuff from him.

Advertisers are trying to sell products. They don't deliberately send messages that will undermine their relationships with the moneybags in their market.

Advertisers are trying to cast themselves as credible and trustworthy folks. They don't intentionally sabotage their own images in the eyes of the public.

But they do it all the time. And unless an ad triggers a flurry of outraged calls and letters, advertisers keep right on whistling while they work, while consumer confidence erodes. Most of the time, advertisers just don't *know* about the subtle bad news, the contradictions their ads might be advertising along with what they hope is the good news about a product.

CHAPTER 4

VICARIOUS AGGRESSION

Philip is fastidious. He sports a neatly trimmed mustache on his upper lip, a crisp white oxford shirt, and freshly ironed jeans. Philip is a free-lance writer with a modestly appointed downtown office. At the end of the day, he dusts the top of his desk. There is nothing left on it but his word processor, telephone answering machine, and one clear Lucite box containing his work-in-progress. Writing implements are safely tucked away in his drawer organizer. Philip returns to an orderly apartment, which his wife, a fourth-grade teacher, keeps immaculate.

People see Philip as a quiet, reserved sort of fellow. He carefully turns over words before speaking, and doles them out as if he were removing neatly nibbled olive pits from his mouth. Philip does not get angry; occasionally, he is "concerned" or "frustrated." But he does not raise his voice, or accelerate the tempo of his speech, or become visibly upset. When Philip experiences "concern," two things happen: One, there is a barely perceptible clenching of his jaw muscles, and two, his face flushes briefly. That's it.

Philip came to see me because he has observed in himself an increasing concern about being contaminated by the germs of others. He finds himself washing his hands after pushing the elevator button in his office building, and has taken to walking huge distances in order to avoid the close proximity of people in public transit. It's not that he dislikes people, he hastens to point out, it's just that he's not *certain* about their cleanliness. It's not that he's saying he's *better* than they, it's just that he takes pains with his personal hygiene, whereas others might not. Despite his vigilance, Philip is secretly afraid that he might, as he puts it, "offend someone by emitting an unpleasant odor."

Philip is hell-bent not to be an angry person—not to be aggressive. He's got his emotions packed away in tidy parcels, but underneath it all, he's terrified of losing control. An only child, Philip spent much of his childhood lying on his bed intently reading science fiction while his parents shouted at each other downstairs.

When I asked him how he felt at those times, Philip recalls, "Well, I was always engrossed in a book. Of course, I wasn't *happy* about the arguing, but what could I do? Once, when I was about ten, I came downstairs and told them I couldn't concentrate on my reading with all that noise. My father's face was bright red, and he suddenly grabbed me and slammed me against the living-room wall and told me to mind my own business. He'd never done anything like that before. I remember seeing him sweat and feeling it drip on my arm. It wasn't too pleasant. I decided right then I was never going to be like him." Is he angry with his father? "No, not really. Frustrated and scared," Philip answers, "but that's in the past now."

So Philip is terrified of losing control. Aggression is as natural an instinct to humans as it is to leopards. But leopards aren't in the business of creating and sustaining a civilization. That's our job, and Western society is built largely on the repression and psychological rechanneling of our innate aggressive impulses. Which means that it's fine to surpass the competition in work and sports, but not fine to kill and eat the competition.

Most of us can get angry but not become homicidal, and can admit that we feel this way without being devastated by guilt. What about Philip? Unfortunately, Philip, whose mother used to tell him he was a "softy from the beginning," got dealt a dad with a nasty temper. He also got dealt an indelible reminder of the retaliation he could expect if he dared to express any real anger. So Philip seals up his feelings as tight as the lid on a Mason jar. *He's* not contaminated by aggressive thoughts—*he* takes extra precautions to cleanse himself as thoroughly as possible. But the people on the subway and in the elevators—*they're* dirty; *they're* sweaty; *they're* angry. And if *he* loses control and perspires—if *he* offends—Philip is afraid that he will be attacked and destroyed in return.

Philip is an extreme, an unusual example of the culturally sanctioned disowning of aggression that is endemic to our society. People, in general, don't like to see themselves as having destructive urges toward their own species, and some go to great lengths to distance themselves from such feelings. One clever way the unconscious performs this trick is through condescension, the holier-than-thou routine, Philip's favorite. One of the oldest in the book, this particular trick is an integral part of the foundation of the advertising that powers the multibillion-dollar deodorant industry in this country. Which brings us to Dial soap.

When Dial was launched in 1948, it was introduced to a world in which very few people used any kind of deodorant at all. It was, as you might expect, a more odoriferous world, but a civilized world nonetheless, in which aggression still bowed to repression. The tagline for Dial's first ad campaign capitalized brilliantly on its market's need not to offend, to see itself as pure of heart: "Even nice people perspire—now the nicest people use Dial." Sounds as if they were singing Philip's song.

By the early 1950's, Dial had harnessed the power of condescension in the theme line "Aren't you glad you use Dial? Don't you wish everybody did?" And the company was off on a winning streak in which the brand has been the biggest-selling deodorant soap for all but two of its forty years in America's tubs and showers.

By 1979, when DDB Needham got the Dial account, the agency's consumer studies had made it clear that people were so familiar with Dial's theme line that when they heard the self-satisfied "Aren't you glad you use Dial?" they mentally filled in the part that wasn't all that nice, the part that was even a little bit supercilious, even aggressive—"Don't you wish everybody did?" Thus armed with "findings" from market research, DDB Needham dropped what appeared to be an unnecessarily overt edge to the campaign and created a series of commercials that did the job all right, but ended up looking pretty much like all the other stylized boy-meets-girl fairy tales selling soap on the tube. Without that zinger, "Don't you wish . . . ," Dial lost some of its psychological power.

By 1986, Dial's banished zinger was returned, along with its emphasis on the soap's deodorizing benefits. In DDB Needham's latest series of commercials, Dial asks us to lather up, put a shine on our superiority badges, and take a seat on a crowded commuter train. In the spot, called "The 5:22," we see the slightly appalled face of a businessman look toward us out the window as the train lurches and the conductor's voice announces the "short delay," after which Dial's famous line occurs: "Aren't you glad you use Dial? Don't you wish everybody did?"

How are the gritty, true-life adventures of the deodorized commuter in Stenchville faring? According to Bruce Delahorne, Dial's account supervisor at DDB Needham, since the spots have been running, sales are climbing and brand awareness is up. What could be better? Well, there's a problem—or so the company thinks.

Apparently, people are receiving the ads with "less pleasure." Why? It's that zinger. DDB Needham's research showed people taking exception to the "Don't you wish everybody did?" bit. Consumers verbalize their dislike for the line and make comments to the effect that they shouldn't tell people what to do, because if they smell, they are within their rights. But do they chuckle at the commercials? Yes. Did they laugh at the zingy tag line? Yes. What's really going on here?

For one thing—guilt. People, and that includes the rarer varieties like Philip, don't like to admit (or don't even know) that they *do* feel angry at people who stink. But that's not very nice. It's much nicer for a consumer to tell a nice market researcher that "Don't you wish . . ." is an unpleasant slur on the inalienable rights of the individual.

Meanwhile, Dial sales and awareness climb. Meanwhile, people are still getting hooked. Going along with the requisite repulsion toward body odor—oh, yes, we're glad we use Dial—we can safely identify with the successfully odor-obliterated Dial user in the commercials. From a position of fragrant security, we can cast scathing glances at nonusers—yes, we guiltily admit, we *do* wish everyone did. Prepackaged, vicarious condescension qualifies as one of our more socially acceptable alternatives to homicidal rage.

Socially acceptable doesn't necessarily mean guilt-free. In the civilized world, guilt is aggression's nagging parent. "How could you even think such a thing? Two wrongs don't make a right. Just count to ten and walk away," chorus the harbingers of guilt if aggression strays too far from its cage of civility. Ironically, the connection between guilt and anger sets off a psychological chain reaction. Anger begets guilt; guilt begets anger. Unfortunately, Commodore International didn't realize this when it ran the in-famous "Train" spot for Commodore 64 home computers, a classic example of the commercialization of guilt.

In "Train," created by Ally & Gargano, the scene opens with the ebullient optimism of the parents of a chunky young man as they put him on a train for college. The announcer informs us, "This year, two million families will send their kids off to college . . . but many of these kids won't be able to compete because they lack computer skills." Uh-oh. Could it be that these osten-sibly caring, responsible parents are really so mean, stupid, and selfish as to not tuck a little Com-modore 64 into Junior's trunk? We learn the sobering truth soon enough. A defeated Junior steps off a returning train. He's flunked out. Junior may be all washed up, but as the announcer's parable draws to a close—"Instead of *saving* for your kid's education, maybe you should *spend* a little for it"—we see the world's best parents in the throes of a festive birthday party as they present a darling little girl with her very own Commodore 64.

According to Julie Bauer, director of advertising and marketing for Commodore International, "Train" was considered a success; 3 million Commodore 64s were sold and "people remember it." As she puts it, "It was the prime time to do that commercial. Both heads of households were out working; you've already got them feeling guilty. They weren't home to take care of Johnny—better buy him a computer. Every manufacturer of home computers was using guilt; we wanted to try a twist, and the idea was to throw a little humor in." At the time, new products were coming out all the time, and fast; it was critical to get advertising out there in front of consumers before the competition got a head start. Ms. Bauer continues, "You had to operate more from gut instinct than anything else—there just wasn't any time to do research."

Humor? I didn't get the joke. The story in "Train" wasn't played broadly enough to be truly funny, and the people in the spot came across as being well-meaning and sincere, but not very sophisticated. Were we supposed to laugh at their ignorance? At the fat flunky? The spot rankled me. I don't believe it sold computers for Commodore because it was humorous. I think it sold computers by holding up a portrait of the kind of ordinary, naive people nobody wants to be and by cranking the ready chain of guilt and inadequacy performance-conscious parents regularly hang around their necks as they scramble to fit their kids into their schedules. It hit a nerve, too, because parents were anxious about giving their kids a competitive edge in the computer age, an age of technology that most parents hadn't mastered themselves. It sold computers by positioning the Commodore 64 as the kind of fast fix Americans have come to expect in product promises. Guilty about not having enough time—quality or otherwise—to spend with your kid? Scared your kid won't make it? No problem. Just buy this gadget (pop this pill) and you'll soon feel those pangs fade away.

"Train" went for a quick-and-dirty short-term marketing gain and bet right. But what about the long-term effects of guilt strategy? Advertising like this just reinforces the stranglehold guilt has on people's lives; it just holds out more ways for them to feel as though they're not measuring up.

Guilt *is* a powerful motivator, but advertisers who attempt to ride it to the market had better do so in a bulletproof car. Eventually, people get angry when they feel jerked around by their guilt. And it's not a good idea to get people mad at you if you want them to let you into their living rooms and want them to go buy expensive stuff from your store. The folks at Ally & Gargano didn't mean to tell parents they were rotten—they just wanted to motivate them to buy computers for their kids' own good. And, of course, the company's.

Advertisers are people who get angry just like the rest of us. And they don't like to see the seamier parts of themselves, just like the rest of us. And, just like the rest of us, they are capable of launching attacks, consciously or not, under the rubric of motivating others to do something for their own good, or for the good of others.

"Dog Bites," a Public Service Announcement (PSA) for the U.S. Postal Service, intends to send a message to dog owners that will enlist their sympathies for mail carriers under canine siege, and persuade them, as the subhead politely asks, to "Please keep your dog fenced, leashed or confined." But the ad's visual is an in-your-face shot of the business end of a Doberman pinscher. Only it doesn't look quite like a Doberman. It looks like a rabid wolf

on a mission from hell. With ghostly light blazing from its eyes and its oozing nightmare jaws straight out of *Aliens,* the animal lunges at the viewer. Above this menacing montage, the headline states flatly, "Dog bites: painful and costly." This is what I like to call retaliatory advertising, but don't tell that to the postal service.

I learned that Marvin has a pit bull about the same time he told me he keeps a gun under his mattress, just in case. At that point, Marvin had been coming to the clinic for four months. Secretive guy. He'd held down his job as a security guard for six months, the longest he'd held any job since he dropped out of Syracuse as a biology major, and about three times longer than he'd ever been in a relationship with a woman.

After telling me that he had been testing me since the beginning of therapy, and was satisfied that he could now trust me enough to tell me about Slate (the pit bull) and the Smith & Wesson (the gun), Marvin explained, "The dog is my bodyguard and the gun is my social security." Marvin lives in a fairly quiet section of the city. It's the kind of neighborhood that will someday succumb to the inexorable gentrification washing up against its shores, but that still boasts ethnic stoop societies. But Marvin is convinced that he lives in a treacherous world; he wishes he had friends, but he's afraid to let down his guard and get close to anyone. When I see the "Dog Bites" ad, I think of Marvin. And I think of how off-base the postal service was in trying to reach *that* audience.

The way to get someone like Marvin to chain Slate up (and I give it a .001 percent probability of effectiveness), is to convince him—somehow—that the world is a less threatening place than he believes. Marvin is not the only owner of a big dog with big teeth and a big rep who feels justified in having this kind of self-protection. The violence of the postal service PSA reinforces Marvin's belief that he *could* be attacked at any time. It reinforces Marvin's belief that he is right in *not* muzzling Slate's massive mandible power. But Marvin should never have been the target of the PSA. No ad could get Marvin to tie Slate down.

By using the image of the Doberman nightmare, the postal service went after an unreachable market. It should have used more benign imagery that could have related to an essentially caring family with a couple of kids and a beloved dog that, despite stern talkings-to, occasionally runs out and impulsively samples a mail carrier. *These* people might be responsive to a heartfelt PSA on behalf of the beleaguered fleet. But not Marvin.

The "Dog Bites" ad is persuasive, albeit not in the way it was intended. But as a justifiably vengeful expression of the mail carriers' fury at being mistaken for a terrorist by somebody's pet grenade, it's a roaring success. But don't tell that to your friendly neighborhood post office. To them, it's—Hey, no offense!—just a rather graphic message put out in the spirit of public service.

Advertising by intimidation reaches reckless heights in Eveready Battery Company's recent campaign for its Energizer brand. "Jacko" Jackson, aka Mark Alexander Jackson, an Australian football player of imposing proportions, is capable of contorting his broad features into a contemporary correlate of the flesh-eating giant greeting Jack at the top of his legendary beanstalk.

In a transatlantic advertising transplant, imported from Aus-

tralia, that never fully took hold in the United States, Jacko's "Fee Fie Foe Fum, I smell the blood, etc." pitching style for the brand evidenced early warning signs of rejection in the initial phases of the procedure.

Essentially, the strategy of DDB Needham's $30 million campaign appeared to be grounded in the Big Bully theory of persuasion. You remember that one—it's part of the core curriculum in elementary school. Say you're at recess and you want to persuade little Gerald with the Twinkies to give you his last one. How can you accomplish this most effectively? Right. Hold your fist to his throat, open your mouth, and bellow your request in his face. It works with Twinkies in the schoolyard—why shouldn't it work with batteries in the supermarket?

For one thing, unlike little Gerald, who is truly a captive audience to coercion, when confronted with the unpleasant tactics of a media Big Bully, we can simply execute the intruder with a swift flick of the channel. In one of Jacko's blitzkriegs, the spiky-haired macho man starts out shouting at the consumer and cranks up the volume from there. "Lasts longer than all the *rest*," he growls, pushing his face up to the screen. Hoisting a huge battery above his head, he thunders, in unison with a chorus of unseen male voices, "The extraordinary Energizer" in what not-so-subtly smacks of a frenetic, hubris-laden advertisement for the awesome prowess of Jacko's special male muscle.

Women were so impressed by Jacko's courtship display that they voted him their "most disliked" celebrity spokesperson in a recent *Advertising Age* survey.

But that's not all. Since Jacko began threatening the U.S. market with Energizer, the brand has lost ground to its archrival, Duracel. What hit the bull's-eye in Australia, a land with the lingering reputation, deserved or not, of having ideas of manliness fixated at the spaghetti-western stage of development, turns out not to be able to hit the side of a barn in New Age America, where men are strong *and* sensitive; where women are strong *and* sensitive *and* can walk away from batteries being hurled at their heads by a Neanderthal. Lately, Jacko's performance in Energizer commercials has been replaced by a little battery-operated rabbit harmlessly pounding away on a tiny drum.

An even more graphic example of the buy-our-product-or-die-sucker school of advertising was an ad that appeared several years ago for a financial institution's risk-management services. Lying on the plush carpet under his desk was the limp-handed, splay-legged, pinstripe-suited body of a ranked company man. A broad beam of light illuminated the trajectory of his collapse. Clearly, the gentleman was not napping. Clearly, the gentleman was dead.

Cause of demise? The poor slob, as you might well imagine, had failed to put his faith in the advertiser and had doomed himself to the heart-stopping stress of an interest rate that put him at serious risk as corporate treasurer. I'll say. I wonder if they also sell life insurance.

When it comes to advertisers bumping off consumers for not using their product, Eclipse Laboratories, Inc., wins the Mortuary Medal. In its ad for Skin Cancer Garde sunblock lotion, developed by I. Goldberg & Partners, a group of well-heeled mourners are shown gathered around the open coffin (for their eyes only) of the dearly departed. How did he go? Skin cancer. How do we know? From the headline: "Here's how you can look with a healthy tan."

In all fairness, both Eclipse Laboratories and its agency were aware of the controversial nature of the ad, and initially ran it only in *Spy,* a definitely off-the-beaten-path magazine originating in New York. Nonetheless, when it is distributed more widely, as the advertiser expects, angry, frightened letters are anticipated. It's fairly clear from this piece of advertising that the company is trying to create a high level of awareness about the product and about the possibility of skin cancer developing as a result of unprotected sun worship. Just look at what it calls itself: Skin (small type) CANCER GARDE (big type).

The problem with this ad is not just its sensationalism; in light of the relative rarity of deadly malignant melanoma, the chances of dying from skin cancer are statistically minute. And it's not just that the ad might be offensive because of its tasteless treatment of death. Apart from the moral and ethical issues involved, as I see it, another very real problem with this ad lies in its misunderstanding of what makes people change their behavior. In other words, it might not even move much product.

In the Cancer Garde ad, the advertiser comes off cloaked in the garb of a rather ghoulish physician, warning the patient—for his own good—of the dangers of disregarding his advice. This is the same type of doc who tries to "help" smokers in his practice by showing them full-color autopsy prints of cancerous lungs. He's only trying, as the Cancer Garde copy echoes, to show you that ". . . there are worse things than not having a tan." How benevolent.

Do these tactics work? Will Dr. Feelbad's portraits in pathology inspire a smog-filled patient to change his polluting ways? Will I. Goldberg & Partners' chilling realization of a bronzed goddess's worst fears—that her years spent living up to Madison Avenue's images of proper skin coloring have turned her into an epidermal time bomb—inspire her to throw herself at the mercy of Eclipse Laboratories and slather herself with Cancer Garde for the few remaining years of her life? No and no.

Getting people to change their behavior—*any* behavior—is a tricky business. And some of the most strenuous mental work all of us engage in, consciously or unconsciously, is the denial of our own mortality. For obvious reasons, thinking about the reality of our last turn at bat—ever—isn't a favorite topic on the human agenda. Considerable effort goes into constructing sturdy defenses against letting information on personal demise into the emotional computer. So, when somebody like Harry, my fifty-two-year-old tailor, whose two-pack-a-day father died of lung cancer, lights up his unfiltered Camel, he's *not* having warning flashes of his very own Dr. Doom's picture show. The Technicolor gore shots don't compute—they're unreal to him. What's real and what's immediate to Harry is having a good smoke.

Behavior change strategies that hold out death threats as incentive have a high failure rate for reasons other than Harry's airtight defense system. When a person's ability to deflect thoughts that are too close for comfort is underdeveloped, the horror leaks in and blows his psychological fuses. There's the initial jolt of emotional overload, and then a shutdown of the mental computer's capacity to process information.

The Cancer Garde ad is a prime-time circuit blaster. Whatever the copy is selling, whatever brand name the consumer is supposed to remember, requires the rational brain to be in gear. But when an ad's imagery is too disruptive, the emotional picture might well be all that is left on the consumers' mental screens.

But enough cringing at advertising's Fright Nite Follies. There's a perfectly acceptable outlet for advertising aggression that has its roots in one of America's cherished cultural pastimes. I refer to boxing. The spectacle of two of the country's meanest machines skillfully pummeling each other into stewed tomatoes gets the seal of society's approval—and makes a fair number of people rich and happy.

Lucky us! We get to have free ringside seats at such on-screen matches in advertising as the notorious Cola Wars in which Pepsi beats out Coke in commercial taste tests, and the great Battle of the Burgers spots where Burger King assails McDonald's—fights that will go down in history and we were there! But did we *want* to be?

Those of us who waited in the lines and bought the tickets and ate the mottled hot dogs and drank the warm beer all for the chance to *be* there when Sugar Ray Leonard finessed a decision victory from Marvelous Marvin Hagler in a fight intensely punishing to both boxers, we wanted to vicariously *feel* the raw power—*wanted* to be there. I watched that historic fight on closed-circuit TV in Jamaica in an open-air theater packed with cheering tourists and locals. I didn't hear anybody debating the ethics of boxing. I didn't hear anybody worrying about Sugar Ray's feelings.

But something different happens when advertising makes an offer to the public for free ringside seats to its competitive brand-slinging campaigns, an offer that it can always refuse by zapping through commercials. Some people get mad and feel that fighting is unfair and wrong. Now, these may not be the people who plunked down sensational scalpers' prices for ninety seconds of Mike Tyson's emulsifying punches, but they *are* the people who buy colas and hamburgers and cars.

Subaru had mixed feelings about the Mercedes-bashing tone of Levine, Huntley, Schmidt & Beaver's ad. There poses the sleek and handsome XT6, set against a brush-stroked background, as if it had sat for its portrait. Beneath its dapper chassis blares the heavy block-lettered headline: "The Kind of Car Mercedes Might Have Built If They Were a Little More Frugal and a Lot More Inventive." It's Subaru calling out Mercedes. It's David calling out Goliath. But they ran it anyway, and they got some flak for it. What kind of flak?

Michael Moore, Levine, Huntley's head of market research, is proud of Subaru's position as a tough innovator. "Subaru's a little bit of a maverick in a positive sense—it pioneered the four-wheel-drive automobile," she says. And the flak? "Whenever you compare yourself, someone pipes up and says, 'I hate it when they put down the other guy.'" All true. When Burger King put down McDonald's, people cried, "Not nice!" And when Pepsi put down Coke, people squirmed; "Not nice!" That's what some people say, but that's not all that's going on beneath the surface.

Name-calling in advertising, a fairly recent development, dares to break a long-standing tacit taboo against using the enemy's name in vain—Big Business lowering itself to engage in the prosaic sticks-and-stones combat of Everyman. Interestingly enough, the most successful hamburger maker in the world, McDonald's, has *never* engaged in competitive advertising. Big Business is supposed to have enough stature and maturity to be above such plebeian ploys. As much as some people might refute this contention—as much cynicism as people express about corporate trustworthiness—ads like Subaru's still generate flak. And they generate flak because some people are still disappointed, because their closely held, largely unacknowledged fantasies of the wisdom and fairness of the American company, like the unconscious belief in the ultimate wisdom and fairness of a powerful parent, are being frayed.

But there's even more than disappointment going on. While the Judeo-Christian's venerable Golden Rule gilds American lips, in the unconscious, it takes a backseat to the longer-running, not nearly as friendly rule, "an eye for an eye." And it's in the unconscious that the story behind the protests to advertising's naming names is played out.

Lynn is a twenty-eight-year-old assistant in a cardiologist's office. Last year she scraped up enough money to buy a snazzy red Subaru. She adores her car. She adores her car a lot more than she adores herself. Lynn is a big woman—5' 7" and 165 pounds—and carries her body as if she were being steadied by the ballast of a loaded shopping bag gripped in each hand. Lynn is always well groomed, from her short, straight brown hair to her clear nail polish, but she's certainly not a fashion plate. With her puffy face and oversized glasses, she falls on the wrong side of the conventional definition of pretty. And no matter how hard she tries to be friendly, she can't seem to get much of a social life going.

Lynn's lifelong nemesis is her petite, happily married kid sister, Catherine. During one of the early history-taking sessions, Lynn recalls, "I never felt what *you people* like to call 'sibling rivalry.' " No? Then I better get set for being on the firing line, I thought to myself as I ducked her "you people" shot. "To me," Lynn says smiling, "Catherine arrived like a wonderful new present for my third birthday. Of course, I guess I didn't like it when she got away with things and I didn't. But that's only natural—she was littler. Well, she stayed littler. Not me. I took after my dad. By the time I was twelve, I blew up—and there was Catherine, cute as a button and skinny as a rail. My mother never raised her voice—no one ever did in my family—but she made it plain that I could 'be a dear' and at least *try* to control my eating—like

Catherine." Bingo. "It's not like I got mad at Catherine—like I said, nobody ever got mad at anybody—but I guess I didn't like being compared like that." Does she feel jealous of Catherine now? Flushing slightly, Lynn says in her pointed "you people" voice, "Not everyone has to feel envious of someone else's good fortune. I try to be happy for her. Anyway, I'm the one who's here, not her. I *suppose* you can help me, even if I *like* my sister." Stepping lightly to dodge another missile, I wonder aloud if Lynn has any idea why people don't warm up to her. "*You're* thinking it's because I'm disgustingly fat," she challenges. No, I'm not. She's not even that heavy. I'm thinking that she has no idea how much hostility comes through in her voice. It sure triggered my radar alert. I can imagine that it sends the people Lynn tries to befriend scurrying for shelter. But Lynn can't understand why she's alone when she tries to be so nice to everybody.

Lynn and I had a way to go in therapy. Along the way, I asked Lynn to do me a favor. I wanted her reaction to the Subaru ad (after all, she's a very satisfied XT6 customer). "This is pretty sarcastic," she began. "They don't have to tear down Mercedes to prove they've got something good. Why can't they just say, 'Subaru is a great car—buy it'?" And then Lynn said what I figured she'd say, because it's perfectly in sync with how she sees herself: "I hate it when they put down the other company. I know this is a weird thing to say about *advertising,* but it just doesn't seem right." It doesn't seem so weird to me. The point is that comparative ads, like Subaru's, are risky for advertisers, but for complicated psychological reasons. Essentially, they reduce already tarnished corporate icons to the tattlings and tauntings of childhood rivalries. And for people like Lynn, and there are plenty of consumers like her out there, it's a lot more comfortable to blame the advertiser for its aggressiveness toward competitors than to face up to the unfinished business of unresolved anger in themselves.

Lately, advertising has been adding an amusing twist. We're being treated to avenues for the vicarious expression of our love-hate relationship with advertising itself. Some advertisers out there are creating ads that actually poke fun at themselves and at the entire industry.

Witness the notorious Joe Isuzu. We've all met him at one time or another in Car Dealership Hell. And, clammy with the memory of adding options that eclipsed "slashed sticker prices" and vacuumed vacation money right out of our wallets, many of us have been powerless to resist his glib gladhandedness. Despite our mistrust of both his patter and his polyester, there are those of us who have shelled out. I know. I was one of the damned.

Wrong.
Prices Start At $6999.

When I first saw Della Femina, Travisano & Partners' "Liar" commercial for American Isuzu Motors, I laughed. Freud was right when he said that jokes are fueled by hostility. As soon as I heard Joe Isuzu's unctuous voice in the spot, I recalled my own recoiling at the toupee-topped grin that greeted me, a naïve twenty-three-year-old, at the Plymouth dealer of my past. "Hi," the well-dressed man with snake-oiled hair intones as the commercial begins, "I'm Joe Isuzu." And then— what a gift!—"He's Lying" appears printed beneath the impostor. And I laughed, thinking about how trapped I felt back then, as I was corralled in an immense lot of cars I instantly loathed, by a character who looked like the sort who'd spend his off-hours sitting under a trench coat at an X-rated movie.

The spot continues with Joe Isuzu claiming one outrageous feature for the car after another, such as "A breakfast nook!" followed by translations such as, in this case, "Split fold-down rear seats." The commercial closes with Joe's toady reassurance, "And if you miss eight or nine payments, that's okay. *I* trust you"—to which the disclaimer enjoins, "Your bank may feel otherwise." And I laughed, as I saw myself signing an agreement for more money than I'd ever intended to spend, trading in an aerodynamic, space-age Plymouth Barracuda for a Scamp, the kind of boxy, serviceable car I'd never dreamed of owning, and listening to Sleeze Incarnate telling me, "Young lady, you're not going to get a better deal than this, take my word."

Who would ever think that a car manufacturer would sit still for—let alone finance!—a parody of its own industry's contributions to the Creeps Hall of Fame. Certainly not the consumer.

And the Isuzu parodies didn't just surprise and entertain. They sold cars. And as I see it, they continue to sell cars because the spots work by what I call "judo advertising." American Isuzu Motors holds up the magnificently crawly Joe Isuzu, the salesman you love to hate, as an irresistible target for the derision we feel thoroughly justified in venting. The advertiser colludes with us, takes potshots right along with us, and then eases us right into the arms of the one we can *really* trust—American Isuzu Motors.

Despite the campaign's deluge of creative awards and marketing successes, it doesn't receive unanimous accolades in the advertising community. A few voice the worry that it besmirches the already dubious image of salesmanship in this country. Shades of the virtually unbreakable rule among physicians never to blow the whistle on one of their own.

So advertising can offer a powerful vicarious outlet for aggression—sometimes conscious, sometimes unconscious—ours *and* even the advertisers' own aggression. Advertisers who ask us to insult clods like Herb, who don't use their product, and to sneer along with them at their competitors, all the while winking at us with fine-tuned flattery, suggest we're on the winning side of a collusion. We're made to feel that the advertisers are letting us in on the game, inviting us into their private club, telling us we and they are part of the same clever, superior team.

In something like judo advertising, an agency like Della Femina's gets to hoist the albatross of advertiser hype with its own petard once in a while and release some residual aggression of its own. Some of that aggression is distilled from those inevitable moments in an agency's life when capitulation to the client's coveted ideas on what sells, however questionable, is deemed more prudent than blowing the account over a disagreement. And we consumers get to rail vicariously against years of advertisers' relentless assaults on our intelligence by laughing through our teeth when the joke's on *them*.

I like judo advertising because it doesn't take itself as seriously as most. I like to be around people who can laugh at themselves; some of the best comedians make fun of their own neurotic behavior. But not everyone can pull it off. Some agencies, like some people, turn their anger into humor effectively and get people on their side in the process. Others are stiff and defensive and embarrassed about calling attention to their own foibles, and end up admitting defeat on the mat as victims rather than victors in the art of judo. After all, a sense of humor can't be legislated in a relationship any more than it can be legislated in a marketing plan.

CHAPTER 5

TELL ME A STORY

Without opening their mouths, people tell stories about themselves all the time. And I don't just mean in body language. America's second tongue is "product language." The latest slang spreads epidemically, largely ignoring regional boundaries; for example, the Harley-Davidson motorcycle, with its air of danger and rebellion, is part of the current product language of the power elite. Malapropisms are sniffed out and scoffed at almost instantaneously by the most facile speakers. Proper nouns become improper overnight.

The final authority on our new language isn't Webster's, it's advertising. And Americans are probably its brightest students, quickly soaking up the vocabulary of different products and using them in complex sentences to flesh out their definitions of who they are.

Advertising's dictionary has it all over Webster's in the fun department—no wonder product language has taken off—just look at what Webster's offers: tiny, complicated print, incomprehensible abbreviations, and no story. Now, consider advertising: big, bold headlines, glorious full-color pictures, simple phrases, and enticing tales. No contest. Advertising sells exciting new definitions of who we are, and all people need to do to buy an identity is to buy the product. The language speaks for itself.

In order to understand Webster's definition of "automobile," we don't need to know how the word originated in order to begin using it in everyday speech. Similarly, in order to understand advertisers' prepackaged portraits of different cars, we don't need to investigate *why* or *how* they arrived at a particular definition. But if we're going to understand product language, the language that we've been exposed to all our lives and that has become automatic to us, we *do* need to figure out the *meanings* themselves. Because that's what we're left with—not the advertiser's intentions, not the agency's creative strategy, not the market research—just the illustrated dictionary of product language called advertising. So what are we *really* buying when we buy an "automobile," which Webster's defines as "a car, usually four-wheeled, propelled by an engine or motor that is part of it, and meant for traveling on streets or roads"?

I know what Kevin bought when he got his Jaguar XJ-6. He told me.

At forty, Kevin heads his own health-care supply company, works long hours, and is fairly successful. Over the past year or so, he has begun to worry if he is having a "midlife crisis." When I ask him what that is, he obligingly tells me, "I've been feeling like—here I am, I'm forty. I have a terrific wife who looks great. But I married her when we were both in college together, and I just wonder if I gave myself enough time to look around. Not that I don't love her—Marion's a great mother to our kids and she does wonderful work at the hospital. I just feel like I'm missing something."

Marion is a stunning, athletic physician specializing in infectious diseases. Kevin is a kind, sweet guy who struggled through the academics of his MBA but came into his own with on-the-job acumen. He was never stunning, and is now losing his hair.

Marion is crazy about Kevin. Kevin has never quite understood why, but wasn't about to question his good fortune. I ask Kevin more about what he thinks he's missing. This isn't easy for him. I can see how uncomfortable he is talking about his personal life with a psychologist—and a woman at that. I notice him twisting his wedding ring as he says softly, "Marion always knows who she is and where she's going. I just know about business. Maybe I'm worried I'm missing something she's got."

Which brings us to the car. When Kevin left his thirties, he decided to do two things: First, he let Marion talk him into getting some counseling for his midlife mopeyness, and second, he traded in his Olds for a Jaguar. Why a Jaguar, you ask? So did I. "I don't know," says Kevin. "I just liked it. I make enough money, and I wanted to indulge myself. I'm not exactly the Maserati type." What type is that? "Greasy, macho, seductive," Kevin answers.

Later that day, I riffled my files and pulled out an ad for Maserati. Kevin was absolutely right—he's not the type. Angling its glowing headlights down from on high, the red Maserati is poised in the blackness above the advertiser's definition of its product's identity: "Power Corrupts. Absolute Power Corrupts Absolutely." The Advertising Dictionary further defines its subject in the body copy: "In the Italian Renaissance the word for power was Machiavelli. In the second Italian Renaissance, the word is Maserati."

Kevin's definition of power as a manager is being able to delegate enough work to people he trusts so that he and Marion can go sailing on the weekends. No, Maserati isn't a part of his product language any more than Machiavelli is one of his heroes.

Not-Maserati still didn't tell me what Kevin's Jaguar meant to him. Kevin is good with words, so I ask him to tell me a story. I ask him to tell me a story about how a man might feel when he drives his new Jaguar, and to tell it as if he's writing a movie script. At first, Kevin seems puzzled and protests weakly that he's not that creative. Then I see him looking off in the distance, as if he's picturing a memory, and he smiles. Here's the story Kevin told me:

> Okay. There's this hard working businessman— not bad looking, but not really handsome. Maybe laying in a bit of a paunch. And all his life he's bought practical, reliable cars that did just what cars are supposed to do, get you from one place to an-

other. Well, finally—he doesn't know why, but he's happy about it anyway—he buys himself a very classy, very expensive British racing green, Jaguar. He's got it parked in a spot outside his office where he can see it from his window on the fifth floor. It looks like a painting—and he shudders when he realizes that it's *his*. He can't wait to get inside it again. When he does, he feels insulated, almost aristocratic. Driving along, he sees people on the sidewalk stare. He's surprised when he admits it to himself, but he likes the status and he likes the attention. He likes thinking that he's being looked at as rich and as important. He feels sexy.

"What a transparent trick!" Kevin admonishes when he finishes his story. "You did that just to get me to talk about myself!" Right, I confess. And when Kevin learned about what he was trying to say with his Jaguar, it gave him a handle on what he felt was "missing" in his life. Not long after that, counseling started to click for Kevin. He still loves to slip behind the wheel of his Jag, but it's no longer the place he feels most viable. Now, he doesn't park that side of himself when he parks his car.

Unlike all the other decorative trappings, unlike all the other kinds of product language people use to declare who they are, our car is the only kind of societal costume we wear that covers us completely. When a driver steps into his car, he steps into a total body suit. Closing the door to the outside world, a driver can operate his disguise safely behind his persona—chosen by him, constructed by advertising—secure in the cabin of his control.

Americans have always engaged in love affairs with their cars and used them to project their own self-images. But lately the old love affair's becoming more symbiotic as society becomes more depersonalized and technology continues to advance on its creators. People feel lonelier and less significant. It isn't just Kevin's midlife crisis that left him feeling empty. It's the country's midlife crisis as we try to grab some inner peace while scrambling to maximize our achievement potential, our sexual potential, our parenting potential, and our longevity potential as we drink only in moderation, munch our way through oat bran muffins, and wear SPF 65 on our dead-of-winter vacation to St. Thomas.

People are looking to feel more alive, to be more in touch with themselves rather than with their possessions or their achievements. Well and good, but from advertising's vantage point (directly in front of the cash register) this search for identity has all the earmarks of a trend, which means market the hell out of it before it fades!

For decades, advertisers have defined automobiles as animals, and implicitly invited buyers to identify with them. We've had Cougars, Impalas, Pintos, Mustangs, Spiders, Colts, Skyhawks. Car advertisers are using the same basic lexicon today, but with a special tip of the hat to the "trend" toward personal growth and development. Today, cars are evolved life forms that consumers can not only identify with—they can *merge* with—on a whole range of levels from the visceral to the intellectual.

Kevin could have chosen to be a shark on his way to his self-identity. He chose a Jaguar. It looks like a good match. Jaguar Cars and its agency, Geer, Du Bois, have brought back its popular and salesworthy jungle-cat theme and revitalized it by setting its "strong silent sensual" animal in a simpler time, in the surreal primitivism of Henri Rousseau. Recently, like so many cars, this Jaguar's not merely a technological advancement—it's not even a car—it's an "evolution of the species."

Verbally and visually, the ad paints a fantasy of smooth control and integration of the primitive, jungle-side of man. People like Kevin, Jaguar's target, identify with qualities that are specific to

this animal myth, personality characteristics and behaviors that are substantively unique, different from other ad-evolved species in automotive engineering, such as Chevy's sharklike Beretta.

Jaguar makes no waves, is noncombative, does not draw attention to itself. Rather than promising aggression as the reward for identifying with this jungle cat, Jaguar is the car that itself possesses "confidence born of proficiency and power," as the copy states. This is no mere brute. Jaguar touts itself as nothing less than an evolutionary achievement where primitive power has become anthropomorphized into a state of "confidence" capable of giving, in concert with the driver, an "authoritative response." No wonder Kevin, beset with his particular midlife insecurities, bought into *this* call of the wild.

Jaguar's definition of itself tugs at people who eschew macho displays of force, preferring controlled relationships with their emotional instinctual natures, relationships in which they are clearly, but quietly, in charge.

Not so with Chevrolet's Beretta—quite a different chapter in the evolutionary story. In its introductory campaign, what we see dramatically rising out of the primordial waters from which all life emerged, is not, despite its impressively threatening dorsal fin, just a new shark, and it is not "just a new car"; it's, the copy continues, "a new species." Sleek, black, dripping, the Beretta is capable of demolishing even the raciest competitors. Beretta dares to emasculate the likes of the Porsche 928S and Lamborghini Countach 5000S by making them, as the copy states, both "blush a bit" (girlishly?) when faced with its superior .33 drag coefficient.

Inviting its market to identify with, to become, the Beretta, the ad, created by Campbell-Ewald Company, asks consumers to "Put yourself in the unforgettable shape of Beretta" (Body by Madison Avenue). The call resonates with our need as humans to continue to grow and develop, to change and evolve, here translated as a process of leaving the self behind by evolving into a new, and dominant, species. The psychological motivation tapped is a drive for power—a drive often stemming from a carefully guarded inner sense of helplessness and vulnerability. For this psychological target, Beretta promises a very sexy benefit: The driver will get in touch with his own animal instincts; he can "turn that raw power into inspired performance" (the consumer hopes it is his own). This is an enormously seductive appeal to those who secretly wish they had a sharper edge and more intimidating teeth at their disposal in life.

In an interesting and profitable shift in imagery, Volvo moves its image higher up on the food chain and capitalizes on our sense of physical vulnerability as humans in the animal world. Rather than offering to gird insecurities with the implied chomping power of a Beretta, Scali, McCabe, Sloves's commercial focuses on the ultimate helplessness of us as humans.

Exquisitely and discreetly shot in soft light, the camera slides over the naked skin of a baby, then that of a man, then a man's hand on a nude woman's back while a woman's voice describes the sorry state of *Homo sapiens* in the wild: "We are the most

complex life form on earth. And yet we are virtually defenseless. We have no claws, no fangs, no protective shell. In fact, our only natural defense is our intelligence." And then the Volvo appears on the screen as the woman continues, "And intelligent people help protect themselves by driving Volvos."

How Darwinian. Volvo is our best defense, the only intelligent choice on the jungle's highway, where survival of the fittest is all too self-evident. How does Volvo define intelligence? As itself. Buy Volvo and you buy what people need to survive—extra IQ points. But there's more going on than Volvo's self-portrait as the Mensa of Motorcars.

Volvo's long-standing, well-deserved reputation is that it's built like an armored car. Lots of intelligent, educated people—with lots of money—buy Volvo, not to make them smarter, but to make them feel as snug as a bug in a bomb shelter. If the bulk of your driving pleasure occurs in a rush of relief at having reached your destination without getting squashed on the road, Volvo is your ticket to ride.

HOW WELL DOES YOUR CAR
STAND UP TO HEAVY TRAFFIC?

VOLVO

Volvo concretizes its consumers' nightmares in a pun-intended ad designed to support the Volvo-as-indestructible image with an unusual demonstration. "How Well Does Your Car Stand Up to Heavy Traffic?" the headline asks intelligent, fearful customers as it shows Volvo as Mr. America (Mr. Sweden?) "supporting the entire weight of a 6¾ ton truck" on its steel shoulders. Now just how bright does a weight lifter need to be? Volvo flatters its consumers' intelligence; but what Volvo is really selling is strength. Volvo will make you invincible. And despite its fancy price tag and conservative classiness, that ability to endure is a prime motivator of people who buy Volvos.

Nancy is telling me in a panicky voice about her driving phobia. She's an articulate, goal-directed city planner who refuses to allow her anxiety attacks to stop her from functioning—but she's very miserable.

"I have a little Toyota Celica," she begins, "and I have to drive the expressway to get to my job. I feel like a mouse in the middle of an elephant stampede. I've got these trucks tailgating me and boxing me in on both sides. There's no place to go and they're looking down on me in this matchbox I drive, and guess who's expendable? I wish I had a tank. I feel so crushable and I get so scared. I hate living like this. I wish I could afford a Volvo. *That's* built like a tank. I know so many people who should be dead now who were in Volvos and walked away from the accident. My brother-in-law cracked up two Volvos and only lost his front teeth. But where am I supposed to get that kind of money? I feel like I'm never going to get over this driving thing. Maybe I should stop coming to therapy and save my money for a Volvo."

Since we figured it would take years for the money she would have spent on therapy to accumulate sufficiently to buy the Volvo, Nancy decided to stick around and try some antiphobia strategies.

She was very conscientious, practiced imagery and relaxation techniques at home, and was able to handle the anxiety before it got under full sail when she plunged into the thundering herd each morning. What did Nancy's highway mastery do to her desire to be ensconced in the hold of a Volvo? Nothing. She's simply established a new goal for herself in therapy: to make enough money to make her next car a Volvo. So much for mind over matter!

As far as that goes, in William Esty Company's ad for American Motors Corporation's Jeep Wrangler we're introduced to

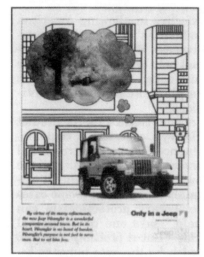

the concept of mind over *metal*. Parked in a line drawing of a city street, we see a full-color photo of the vehicle *daydreaming* a full-color photo of itself in the forest. Jeep lives—and not as a dumb "beast of burden," the copy asserts. Jeep lays claim to powers of imaginative thinking. Although it needs, like its target consumer, to be able to function in the colorless, cartoonlike world—"around town" —of everyday life, Jeep literally daydreams a picture of its true roots in nature.

The message is that, by taking Jeep on, not as a vehicle, the copy rhapsodizes, but as "a wonderful companion," the instinctual self, the wood nymph, as it were, in the consumer will be "set . . . free" from the sterile shackles of urban obligations.

Jeep has gestated, not into any old human, but into a fantastic, enlightened being capable of far more than simple servitude. In fact, the ad goes so far as to paint a portrait of the consumer as the longing, daydreaming Jeep itself—already united in symbiotic bliss. By personifying its target as the car being marketed to him, the ad bypasses logic and immediately conveys its message of understanding what the consumer really needs—what he really wants. Implicitly, the advertiser praises its target: It knows you have a heart; you can tell because the Jeep is painted heartthrob red, an image of creative escapism done up in living color. The ad is a playful piece about a playful vehicle; both are telling the consumer to come back to his senses and start living. How? By buying the car, of course.

Jennifer is one of those yearners-to-be-free who bought the Jeep—bought the fantasy—and made it her own. Jennifer is a woman whose life has always been so complete and so comfortable that she's bored most of the time. She wishes things were more exciting and more adventurous for her. She was raised in a comfortable suburban development in a comfortable suburban split-level, grew up, got married, and now lives in a comfortable suburban condominium. Jennifer manages a framing store in a mall three miles down the road from her home. Three miles to get there; three miles to return to her mondo-condo. If she has shopping to do, she does it at the same mall where she works.

Jennifer used to undertake this commute behind the wheel of a Dodge. "I never realized how boring that drive was," she confided, "until the Dodge broke down and I started looking at new cars. I don't know how it got into my head, but I saw this Jeep and I *had* to have it. My parents thought I was nuts—you know, what are you going to do with *that* thing, Jennifer, drive through the woods to get to work? But my husband was on *my* side. Anyway, I bought it and it's amazing. When I get in the Jeep in the morning, I actually *feel* different. I'm all dressed up for work—the dress, the heels, the bag—but I feel like I'm going camping or something. Not that I'd ever *do* it, you understand. But it's a little like I'm roughing it. I feel like it makes me kind of unpredictable—like what's *Jennifer* doing in a Jeep? At least I don't feel so boring. It adds a whole other side to me. Even if it is only for a little while." Jennifer's Jeep is pure fantasy. Well, not strictly speaking—it does have a practical function as transportation. But the way Jennifer talks about it, she's in dreamland. Why did she pick a Jeep to define herself?

Jennifer was never very rebellious as a child, but she did have an affinity for nursing small, damaged animals back to health in her basement, an avocation her mother found repugnant. After enough parental preaching on the debilitating diseases she could contract as Florence Nightingale to the neighborhood's turtles, birds, and bunnies, Jennifer finally retired her nature-girl calling and went on with the business of being a dutiful daughter. I believe Jennifer's Jeep resonates with her squelched earthiness, and is especially dear to her because her parents disapproved of the purchase. It's her stab at rebelliousness and her stab at playing nature girl again; she's internalized Jeep's advertising image enough to daydream herself, however briefly, into a more exciting identity.

With American Honda Motor Company's advertising for its Accord, the advertiser offers not just a temporary personality shift; it promises a total mind-body meld with the car. Although the ad claims that "it was no easy operation," Honda's startling announcement that now "Your hipbone's connected to our wishbones" is nothing short of miraculous, even in today's extraordinary environment of cars evolving from their atavistic beginnings into modern species of their own. Consumer consent to be surgically linked with the Accord is irrelevant—the procedure is presented as a *fait accompli:* "We made history," the copy declares. Honda as Frankenstein.

Although Honda plays the physician with a hint of the macabre, the script shows superb attention to the traditional posturings of the doctor role. Consumers are reassured with regard to the anesthetic (". . . maybe you won't feel anything"), encouraged to be grateful, and referred to as bodies ("your anatomy will thank our engineering"), even spared data too complicated for the layman ("by-passing the technical term . . .").

With its image of the advertiser as transplant-surgeon extraordinaire, created by Rubin, Postaer & Associates, the ad capitalizes on one of our cherished rituals—the culture's knee-jerk genuflection to physicians. By generating its self-image as one of these highly respected authority figures, Honda distances itself from being just another mundane (crass?) car dealer. As the wielder of higher clout, Honda hopes that its claim to have "connected" the consumer to the wishes—to the very "wishbone"—of the advertiser, will gain credibility with its audience. And, of course, the wishes Honda makes on that wishbone are that this market of "hipbones" will buy their cars.

THE MERCEDES-BENZ 190 CLASS
RESCUES THE SPORTS SEDAN
FROM ITS PROLONGED ADOLESCENCE.

Engineered like no other car in the world

In contrast to the car-as-driver approach in Honda's Accord ad, Mercedes-Benz of North America posits car-as-therapist-for-driver. Created by McCaffrey & McCall, Inc., the ad's headline above a full page of print proclaims, "The Mercedes-Benz 190 Class Rescues the Sports Sedan from Its Prolonged Adolescence." Mercedes-Benz's market has to have made it big enough to afford the high-priced spread, and these tend to be folks busy fighting off the insulting encroachment of middle-age spread. For the rest of the story, Mercedes-Benz smooth-talks its way into consumers' egos, telling them, almost hypnotically, in soothing, supportive therapeutic language, that it's *okay*. The copy suggests that to have mellowed from the halcyon days of youthful vigor to "a welcome change from the edgy machismo" is *okay* because, as Dr. Mercedes-Benz soothingly reassures, "This automobile accepts you for who you are . . ."

Whose "prolonged adolescence" is Mercedes really talking about? It's not that of the other "sports sedans"—it's that of Mercedes's middle-aged customers themselves. And it's in the advertiser's own best interest to set the treatment goal for its market as a greater appreciation of its maturity. Dr. Mercedes-Benz wants its patients to know that it's *okay* to give up the old battles for the sake of the greater, more spiritual pleasures of maturity: "It almost mystically transforms the act of spirited driving from a state of adolescent rebellion to a state of exhilarating civilization."

Dr. Mercedes-Benz sounds a bit grandiose; but then, the good doctor's bag is to set himself up as the lifeline out of a lingering adolescence. Without the therapeutic rescue mission, the rich, middle-aged consumer would be doomed to an existence as a "frustrated racer" instead of experiencing, as the copy promotes, "that liberating sense of driving by mature and uncanny instinct." Oh, Dr. Mercedes-Benz, what a flatterer you are!

Come on, Mercedes-Benz. People are too savvy to believe this kind of image-making. Aren't they? I asked Michael, a forty-six-year-old internist, why he traded in his BMW for a Mercedes. Michael prides himself on, among other achievements, watching cable and PBS channels almost exclusively, so that he can avoid all commercials. I fully expected him to specify the advantages of certain Mercedes features over BMW's. What I got back was practically a commercial on his new car's image. "The BMW was a fine car, but there's no comparison. I don't know how to explain this, but I feel like I'm finally old enough to have a Mercedes. Not that I feel old, but I'm certainly not a kid anymore. It *is* in a class by itself." Michael, the ad-hater, falls under the spell of Madison Avenue's Mercedes, cloaks himself in grown-up grandeur, and drives confidently off into the sunset.

If Mercedes-Benz is out there parading around as the zenith of automotive maturity, who is the flag-bearer of raging hormones? With a headline like "In Thrust You Trust," with the elongated hood of the red Supra surging upward, Saatchi and Saatchi's ad for Toyota's Supra makes a fairly strong case for its inclusion in the gonad gang. Yes, this Supra is all man and it doesn't need to be rescued, thank you. Stand back and give it room—it takes no prisoners. The ad's copy cuts straight to the crux of the matter for its overheated target market: "To own the 1988 Supra Turbo is to own the road. . . . this isn't mere street theater, it's electrifying performance. . . . Rule in comfort."

This is exactly the type of obvious show of machismo that Michael disavows in his Mercedes, and exactly the type of thing Fred, his tennis partner, would like to display. Fred and Michael are the same age, and both play decent tennis, but that's where the similarity ends.

Fred has no interest in curbing the adolescence he feels he finally got a taste of after his divorce last year. He imagines himself to be quite dashing and eligible now, and has taken to wearing Reeboks with his suit to the office. Fred can get away with it, because he owns the store. Thrust power is just what Fred is looking for in a car. Thrust power is what Fred is looking for in himself. Michael told me recently that Fred calls the Mercedes "the old man" and is threatening to buy a "muscle car" like a Corvette "so he can run me off the road." Different needs, different images—each sure his product language tells the

best story about himself. Neither fully grasps how real the tales
have become.

What about people who have no interest in streaking by the
competition in a performance car and feel no attraction to the
understated European status cars? What about people who want
to drive a big car and get noticed, and aren't shy about admitting
it? If impressing others is on your wish list for cars, the Lincoln
Town Car wants *you!*

You want big? Uniworld Group, Inc.'s ad for Lincoln-Mercury's
Town Car grandly flaunts itself across a double-page magazine
spread. While other American cars have been busily trimming their
bulging figures over the years, the Town Car is one that "still
possesses the enduring virtues of this automotive class." Which
virtues? Why, the virtues of "Undiminished size. Uncompromised
comfort. And an unmistakable road presence that separates it dramatically from the rest of the field." The Town Car is a big American fat-cat suit. And lots of people like to wear it.

I used to work with a ten-year-old girl, Donna, who was the
only child of parents who had her late in life. Donna's problems, according to her parents, were that she got "silly" and wouldn't "set-
tle down." As it turned out, these problems could be translated as
"Donna tires us out. Why can't she be more grown-up?" Donna's
father was sixty-three years old, and tall, trim, tailored, and retired.
He drove her to our sessions in an always spotless, long black Lincoln Town Car. I knew it was a Town Car, because he consistently
referred to it by name. "I'll just wait in the Town Car," Donna's
father would say as he walked his daughter to the door.

Donna was dressed up and trotted out for a variety of social
events like benefit dinners and fortieth-anniversary parties as if she
were a precious object. After one of these festive encounters, Donna
would spend a great deal of time in the session making figures out
of Play-Doh and pounding them into the table with her fist.

At regular intervals, I asked Donna's parents to come in so I
could help them understand her as a child and help them, as they
put it, "get her to cooperate." I remember being struck by what
Donna's father wanted his daughter to get out of the counseling
sessions. "Look," he said waving his hand dismissively over my
shelves of toys and materials, "Donna isn't here to play. She's here

to learn that we have certain values in our family and that we expect her to be one of us. We are quite comfortable, and I want Donna to appreciate the good things and the good life we have."

Donna's father talked about her as if she were an investment that wasn't holding its value. He was clearly disappointed in her. And then he said something I could never forget: "Take my Town Car—I drive it to somebody's club and I know I'll be well treated. I don't have to *ask* for anything special—the car says it all. But I take Donna with me to a magnificent party, and she whines that she's bored. And then she spills her soda and cries. That's not how I want her to act."

I wondered, "Why do you take her to these adult affairs if she's so difficult?"

Donna's parents both chimed in on this one, "We want her to learn how to present herself like a young lady. We want her to be able to join us in the things we think are important, and we don't think there's anything wrong with that."

Donna's father would have liked her to be as reliable a token of his prestige as his cherished Town Car, but it wasn't working out that way. She was clearly too willful to be much good in the status department.

Underneath it all, Donna's parents felt painfully awkward and incompetent when it came to dealing with a small child. They weren't so much disappointed in Donna as they were disappointed in themselves. Underneath it all, they wanted to be able to enjoy their little girl but hadn't the foggiest idea of how to go about doing it. They finally got a sense of how different a ten-year-old is from an adult and started to insist less on her attendance at the fetes they had felt were so important. They loosened up in other ways, too, and, as I'd hoped, were rewarded with a happier, more cooperative child.

Recently, I called to check in and see how things were going and Donna's father gave me a brisk, but positive update and then, true to form, announced: "I'm on my way out in the Town Car. I got a new one, you know." No, strangely enough (from his perspective), I didn't know. Donna may be less tied in to impressing others, but her father hasn't quite made that leap. For him, as long as he's able to face the world in his Town Car, he still imagines himself the envy of everyone he meets.

BMW creates its image of ultimate superiority in an entirely different way than Lincoln Town Car does. In a recent commercial created by Ammirati & Puris, a harrowing highway blowout nearly causes a devastating accident. As a truck skids sideways, we hear the heart-stopping sounds of an explosive blowout and squealing tires, as a station wagon careens toward a ditch. A couple in a shiny BMW barrels toward the scene and sharply maneuvers around the catastrophe, narrowly escaping becoming part of the catastrophe themselves. The voice-over underscoring BMW's edge: "Antilock brakes . . . uncanny control . . . sedans built to survive accidents." As the couple leave the scene, we hear them wonder aloud, "Maybe we should go back and see if they're all right."

The BMW spot sounds as if it's built around a safety message, doesn't it? Except that when it was distributed to the dealers, the last three seconds of the spot, in which the concern-for-others comment is heard, was cut off in order to add local tag lines, leading to an initially outraged reaction to the spot. The BMW drivers  looked like a couple of serious yuppies ignoring the tragedy they had sidestepped. When the advertiser realized that this critical section of the spot was being eliminated, it instructed dealers to run it only if that final message was present. Interestingly, the commercial, run in its entirety, was misinterpreted by some as being a revision of an "original" in which the sensitive musings were added at the end to moderate the impression of aloofness. The speculation was incorrect, but as a car that has billed itself for years as "The Ultimate Driving Machine," BMW isn't just selling safety, it's selling snob appeal as well. In the commercial, the BMW *is* completely above it all; it swerves around the disaster as if it's on an altogether different plane of reality—a higher plane. In that situation, of course, that's the right plane to be on.

BMW is a car of the elite. Another ad that plays on the car's long-standing tagline calls the BMW convertible model "The Ultimate Tanning Machine." It's easy to imagine the discreetly omitted bombshell-in-bathing-suit taking a top-down spin to soak up

THE ULTIMATE TANNING MACHINE.

There are cars without roofs. And then there's the BMW 325i convertible.

Created for the exhilaration of sun-worshippers and high-performance devotees throughout the world, the BMW 325i convertible is, first and foremost, a BMW.

Second and foremost, it is a true, structurally integrated convertible built from the ground up—"unlike some non-factory, sawed-off roof jobs on other makers' cars" (Motor Trend magazine).

Thus, it offers classic BMW roadhold-

ing and handling, whether chasing the sun up twisted mountain passes or cruising in the glow of a summer-lit highway.

To experience some hair-raising performance—literally—and enjoy a demonstration of "the most perfect go-away

roof yet" (Road & Track), visit your local authorized BMW dealer.

He'll show you how to go from 0 to 60 in 8.6 seconds. (Note: from pale to tan will take you slightly longer.)

THE ULTIMATE DRIVING MACHINE.

some rays. BMW dangles technology with one hand while deftly massaging the status-seekers' narcissism with the other. If the car fits, wear it.

Claudia does. She owns an expensive little French restaurant in an exclusive suburb where money may very well grow on trees. The food is fabulous and, she would hope her clientele thinks, so is Claudia. She's always there to greet her "guests," always remembers names and food preferences, and always looks as if she's about to be discovered. The frosted hair is moussed to military precision, one of her two-toned polished nails is set with a diamond, gold is draped from all available appendages. Recently, I noticed a new license plate on the BMW she parks at the restaurant in a spot with her name on it. I thought it was a perfect fit all around, between BMW and *its* image and Claudia and the image *she* shares with her car: It reads "STARLIT." I guess that's why they call them vanity plates.

What about the people who wish they had the money and the status that a car like BMW could communicate? If you're Hyundai, you could pitch your advertising to the insecurities of these folks and bait your line with tasty tidbits your aspiring target market can brag about to save face with the Joneses. Backer, Spielvogel, Bates, Worldwide's ad for Hyundai makes no bones about playing to its crowd's sense of embarrassed inferiority and offers a host of pretensions consumers can parrot in defense of their purchase. The headline starts out strong on the subject: "$5395. But you don't have to tell anybody."

Just out of the gate, the ad sets the tone for Hyundai's image —a car that will help you conceal your pitiful financial condition. The copy offers a cornucopia of items a consumer can use to

impress others and steer them away from asking about the car's decidedly déclassé price tag. The entire foundation of Hyundai's arguments rests on the assumption that consumers buy cars to sell images of themselves—and Hyundai sets about advising them how to play the role of a rich person without being unmasked.

First of all, the copy promises, "When people see your new Hyundai Excel, they'll probably think you spent a lot of money." Whew! And first impressions *do* matter when it comes to image-making. But, the copy encourages, there are "plenty of things to talk about besides price."

The lessons in deception go on to teach the consumer how to direct attention to the car's features, instead of to the price: "You can start by telling people . . ."; "And be sure to point out . . . and casually remark . . ." Hyundai is only trying to empathize with the plight of the budget conscious, image-hungry consumer by offering a script. Isn't that what Americans are about, the ad seems to say, bragging about their cars? The price, and Hyundai will understand "if you don't want to talk about it," will be, the advertiser coos ingratiatingly, "our little secret."

Hyundai's sell-to-the-insecure approach may be blatant, and arguably may carry a dash of irony, but it represents a bare-bones look at an advertiser playing on a need to impress that it helped create in the first place. We affect advertising and advertising affects us. Hyundai isn't a Mercedes-Benz or a Town Car or a BMW— it would never be confused with the kind of cars people buy in order to wow others with their social status. But the advertiser still wants a piece of that motivational action, even from Hyundai buyers who are after basic transportation that's affordable and that works. So it generates reasons why consumers *ought* to focus on image, even if the image question *isn't* a driving force for them, because image is what drives car purchases. Hyundai won't just sell you a car, it'll sell you a story you can tell yourself and tell your friends, and in that way, it's no different from a Rolls-Royce.

CHAPTER 6

IN SEARCH OF THE REAL

On he droned, the newly hired hospital head administrator, introducing himself to us, a cadre of overworked, underpaid psychologists and social workers. It was years ago, but I still remember how we stifled a collective groan as this savior of the state's ailing hospital system presented his grand plan to interrupt the proverbial revolving door—in/out/in/out/in—of mental illness.

There we sat, the ones who would be charged with carrying out the impossible mission. There he stood, his fair hair freshly preened, resplendent in his natty brown tweed suit, complete with red plaid vest festooned with watch chain—fairly bursting with enthusiasm for his own ideas. And then, as his remarks finally drew to a close, he looked at us earnestly and announced, "I just want you to know that I'm a *real* person. You can talk to me." Surrounded by the restless stirrings of an audience presented with a patent absurdity, I stifled a socially inappropriate smile.

Here was this guy setting himself up as a visionary, pontificating about implementing complex treatment strategies for chronically ill patients to a staff already turning blue from the daily asphyxiation of bureaucratic red tape—and he pronounces himself a "real person." I remember thinking, if he had to *say* it, he probably felt even more like a phoney than he sounded. When I see advertisers, those for-profit treatment centers for product health, increasingly labeling *their* packaged images as reality, I can't help thinking about that hospital administrator campaigning so hard to convince us he was real that it sounded like false advertising.

Imagine this: an attractive female model, sporting all the trappings of a press photographer, holding her conspicuously poised cigarette above a brand logo. There is enough data there to easily categorize the image as a piece of advertising trying to hook consumers with a picture of how successful, exciting, and seductive a woman could be if only she'd smoke this brand. We've been here before, and we recognize this as typical of the images that pelt us in the daily measuring-up game Madison Avenue summons us to play. But what happens when an advertiser takes this picture, as R. J. Reynolds Tobacco Company did with McCann-Erickson, its recently axed ad agency, in its recent campaign for Winston, and tries to persuade its audience not just to buy its brand of cigarettes, but to buy its image of the model in the ad as "real"? Then the measuring-up game, which we all play whether or not we *want* to, and whether or not we *believe* we do, goes into overtime.

In the Winston piece, the model isn't just being offered as an advertising vehicle, her *image* is being sold and branded itself: She's a product called "Real People." Here's where things can get fairly convoluted. We know that the business of advertising is the business of image-making, but when the illusion is defined as reality, and when we *know* it's far from real—simply because it's advertising—our first impulse might be to reject the whole package as fake. Like the hospital administrator who unconsciously spotlighted his speciousness by trumpeting his genuineness, the Winston ad self-destructs under the weight of its own illusion. Obviously, this is not a real person: It's a model playing a real person. Is Winston's "Real Taste" just as fake as the model who's faking being a real person?

But there's another effect that ripples beneath the surface of what might appear to be an easily dismissed advertising strategy: By calling the woman "real," the Winston piece creates the illusion that the glamorous life of the press photographer is even *more* accessible than if she were permitted, tacitly, to be perceived as simply a model. In a subtle way, this style of advertising intensifies the pressure to measure up, because if she is *supposed* to be "real," just like you and me, the image appears to be more attainable. Implicitly, the advertiser is suggesting that we can be just as comfortably real as this very professionally competent and comfortable-with-herself woman, if we can only imitate the whole role—cigarette and all.

Del Monte plays the reality shell game in an ad for its Fruit Snacks that works on a psychological dynamic similar to the Winston campaign. In heavy black letters, the headline demands that its market of mothers "Get Real," which the copy defines as meaning "Get Del Monte Fruit Snacks," because it has "100% real fruit." But the psychological underpinning of the "Get Real" message is that a *real* mother buys her kids "real," that is, natural and healthful, snacks such as *this* one, and that if she fails to do so, she's somehow less of a mother. But just how real *are* Fruit Snacks? Along with the "100% real fruit," says the Del Monte ads, these snacks possess "other great tasting ingredients." They're not listed in the ad, so I went out and read the back of the box in the supermarket. Here's what I found:

> Yogurt coating (sugar, partially hydrogenated vegetable oil), one or more of the following oils: coconut, cottonseed, palm, palm kernel, soybean, non-fat milk solids, non-fat yogurt solids, dried whey, artificial color, Lecithin, vanillin. Strawberry flavored crunch apples (vacuum puffed dried apples), natural strawberry concentrate, artificial flavoring, sulfur dioxide, sodium sulfite to preserve color, citric acid, artificial color, corn syrup, dextrin, confectioner's glaze.

"I *know* these things are sweet," my friend tells me as she hands her four-year-old daughter a chocolate-covered granola bar, "but at least she's getting something nutritious. It's better than candy."

Del Monte Fruit Snacks' advertising establishes a powerful directive to people, by tapping into their insecurities about being decent, caring parents. It gets parents to measure up to higher snack standards by buying a product that sells them the illusion that it's as real as the strawberries and apple slices surrounding the package in the ad. And consumers play the game, even if they have a certain savvy.

Karen knows her daughter eats the granola bar because it's sweet and chocolate-covered, but at the same time, Karen buys the packaging/advertising reassurance that this stuff is somehow "better than candy." Better because it has more "real" ingredients in it.

When we consumers are playing along with this reality game, we may not believe the advertising, but we're willing to hedge our bets. We don't actually believe the poised female photographer in the Winston ad bears a close resemblance to any real person whom we know, but on the other hand, there's something about her, a worldliness and smartness and sense of adventure, that we would like to believe we share. And we don't actually believe that Yogurt Coated Crunchy Apple Bits are as real as fresh fruit, but on the other hand those Fruit Snacks *might* be just a little bit better than the other kind of sugar-coated fake food that kids like to munch on. As far as the advertiser is concerned, the ad is successful if we (the consumer) feel just a little bit more comfortable with the "real" sweet-flavored snack food than we do with a competitor's even-less-real sweeter-than-sweet product.

Of course advertisers play on insecurities about how we take care of our children. But they also play on insecurities about how we take care of ourselves—what we eat (and smoke and drink), what we wear, and how we look. This all has to do with personal identity, the shakiness of which, as every advertiser knows, consciously or unconsciously, is fertile ground for advertising influence.

Everywhere we look, identities are in crisis, in transition, or in limbo. And when any of us go searching for a new sense of identity, we're likely to go searching for a new product as well. If advertisers can lead us in that search, they will. Trying to sort out the illusions and realities that influence people as they try to sort themselves out from their perceptions is hard work in a consumer society. Marching together through a reality of goods and luxuries, people and products get inextricably entwined.

I am reminded of Sheila, a client I worked with during an important transition in her life. Sheila was a thirty-two-year-old paralegal who, despite her solid good looks and intelligence, hadn't dated much. She made good money, had her own apartment, read extensively, and was still battling with her parents. Sheila's father was a rhino-hide of a Yale lawyer who constantly insinuated that she could have got into his alma mater if she had been smart enough to use his contacts. Sheila's mother called her twice a day, every day, to see how she was feeling. After all, Sheila was still single, so her mother assumed the worst.

When Sheila came to see me, she had got to the point where she didn't know where her parents' programming left off and where her own identity began. But she had an admirable stubborn streak. Though she had not lived up to her father's expectations by turning into a high-powered lawyer, stubborn Sheila had learned so much about the law as a paralegal that she told me she could now one-up her father in conversations about legal issues. She had ways of proving herself to her mother as well. Though still *technically* single, Sheila had a perfectly satisfactory relationship with a man she had been seeing from time to time, whereas her parents had a marriage that seemed to be missing more than a few beats. According to Sheila, her parents had been sleeping in separate bedrooms for years.

But, even though Sheila had been living on her own since college, she was still trying to establish herself as an independent adult. When I think about the complexities of the psychological task we all must tackle—some more consciously and deliberately than others—that of developing a solid sense of who we are, apart from the expectations and obligations we shoulder from childhood, I think of Sheila's solution.

Sheila used to joke with great sincerity about acting being the ultimate solution to the problem of finding out her "real" identity. Since she figured she was just acting on her parents' script anyhow, any role she purposefully chose to take on would necessarily be more real than her current command performances.

And yet her oft-repeated comment to me was "I keep wondering who I really am."

She apologized for wondering. She said she felt like "a leftover from a sixties encounter group," as if the search for a real person were somehow dated, like a pair of bell-bottoms. I assured her it wasn't, that we all engage in a search for identity, a search that goes hand in hand with a search for meaning.

With Sheila I observed how that search took on physical manifestations as her product language shifted. During the time I was seeing her in therapy, she changed hairstyles. Her wardrobe underwent a complete transformation. She began using different kinds of makeup, though generally using less of it. She even switched brands of perfumes. Obviously, and understandably, part of Sheila's identity was tied up in what she wore, how she looked, even how she smelled. And to the extent that she was looking for her "real" identity, she was in search of a new look that would feel "right" (more real) to her.

I wondered what would finally click for Sheila. At what point would she become comfortable with herself—and consequently more comfortable with how she appeared to others? Or would her restless, trial-and-error changes in makeup and wardrobe be an ongoing struggle in her life as she continued to "experiment" with identities?

In a consumer society heavily bombarded with advertising, where people see hundreds of different representations of their own identities, illusion and reality are inevitably blurred. And the pressures of advertising blur the distinctions even further.

"Image" is not imaginary. It is a marketable, identifiable component of successful "real life" in its many and various forms—in professional, romantic, and social terms. Presumably, if Sheila could find the real Sheila and get the look that went along with that real person, identity and image would be harmoniously blended in one. The discomfort of not knowing "who she really was" would dissipate. Sheila-as-seen-by-herself would become one with Sheila-as-seen-by-others.

Advertisers know there are millions of Sheilas out there, and they do everything they can to "help" her find herself. What they promise, in essence, is a higher comfort level, a guaranteed release from the unhappiness or the uneasiness of not knowing who we are. If we can climb into the "real" world offered by advertising, we'll all be confident, competent, successful—free-to-be-us, exceptional but ordinary people in this pressure-cooker world of expectations.

It's a big promise—tantalizing. And in advertising terms, the promise works. Repeatedly.

Consider an ad that came out of Condé Nast Publications. The ad is a true mind-boggler if you try to unravel what the advertiser seems to be saying about reality. On the left-hand sheet of the double-page spread is a photo of the August 1988 cover for *Glamour*, with its usual full-page cover-girl shot. Her complexion is flawlessly made up, any imperfections have been airbrushed out

ce, and she smiles in that model manner that leaves the
wide enough not to cause unsightly crinkles in their corners.
Her brows and lashes have been perfectly penciled and deftly shaded
to highlight her eyes. All the nonverbal cues are lined up to signal
MODEL. But the ad has more to say.

On the right-hand side of the *Glamour* spread, in the same
color and type as the *"Glamour"* headline, are the words "For
Real." Only here, the picture is of a different woman, wearing
exactly the same clothes and hairstyle as the model on the left, but
tag-lined "Real Beauty for Real Women." She's certainly attractive
but, in comparison to the model on the left, shows unmistakable
signs of imperfection. Her skin tone includes a few freckles; when
she smiles, her eyes go along for the ride and lines appear at the
corners around her mouth—dead giveaways of human smiling behavior.

Beyond these nonverbal cues, tracking the advertiser's idea of
reality, as it's communicated through words and pictures, gets to
feel like an exercise in logical contradictions. By separating its real
cover girl from the non–cover girl designated as "For Real," *Glamour* appears to be setting up a contrast between the fabrication of
a model-image and the nonfabricated, "real" woman on the right-
hand side of the page. But who does the advertiser choose as an
example of a real person? *She's* designated "Julie Johnson, Actress."

This is where I start thinking about all the Sheilas who are
already buying *Glamour* and all the other Sheilas whom *Glamour*
considers its consumer market. Like every advertiser who works
on image, *Glamour* is in the business of making women a bit
uncomfortable with who they are, while offering dreams, promises, or guidance that will help them become something more. But
the endless search for ever-more-beautiful models for the cover of
Glamour now goes into quick-reverse. Now, *Glamour* tells us the
model is no longer everything we want and need because she is
not, in *Glamour*'s terms, a "real woman." The *real* woman has
less makeup, more crinkles, and a more genuine, open expression.
On the left is beauty that is only skin deep because it isn't quite
real; on the right is real beauty, without the fake effects of traditional glamorization.

Many Sheilas might be won over with this strategy if it were consumer—instead of media—oriented. Because this might be just what searchers-for-identity want to see. Sheila has seen cover-girl makeup. She's seen enough skin-deep fakery. This ad would tell Sheila she can measure up to *Glamour*'s standards just by throwing on some fashionable, casual clothes and stepping "as is" into the real world, wearing a bright smile and an honest look.

But if we think longer about what *Glamour* is offering, we realize that the advertiser's image of a "real woman" is nothing more or less than Julie Johnson, an *actress*—in other words, someone who makes it her business to play the roles of other characters.

A big problem with advertisers' current appropriation of the reality market is that the effect of labeling an ad's fabricated image as "real" is to immediately conjure up its polar opposite: "fake." The strategy doesn't make marketing sense because if the *ad* comes across as trying to pull a fast one on consumers—honestly folks, this is *real* snake oil—then the *product* ends up with certain snake-oil properties.

The strategy has limited potential, even from a marketing standpoint. Psychologically, people experience what is real to them in highly personal, idiosyncratic ways, and telling another person what she *should* consider real is playing with emotional fire. Meanwhile, people can react on a variety of levels to these kinds of reality puzzles, ranging from feeling vaguely insulted, turned off, or cynical, to feeling anger at the arrogance of advertisers' assumptions. In my experience, most advertisers aren't aware of the range of *psychological* reactions consumers can have to "reality" campaigns. To most, it's just a creative concept.

Looking closely at some ads, you can unravel the threads of their own destruction. Take Levi Strauss's latest serving of reality to the public. San Francisco–based Foote-Cone Belding's ad is a double-page spread composite of thirty-eight black-and-white "snapshots" of women wearing jeans in a variety of resolutely slouchy, Spartan, free-spirited settings, complete with early sixties Cadillac, Goodwill-furnished warp-wooded shore house, and open field. The headline telling us how we ought to interpret this collection of images is "Real Life Wears Real Jeans."

Real life, according to the advertiser guru, is lived by a woman with a propensity for posing in seductively casual disarray, lying facedown across the front seat of a car, or bed, or beach, so as to

present posterior photo opportunities. It all looks studiously or-
chestrated, but Levi's implicitly assures us that the scenes reflect
real life because the shots are all of a model wearing "Real Jeans,"
which, as defined by the advertiser, are what makes life real. But
only if the jeans are real Levi's.

What the ad is actually promising is a vintage convertible, a
hip urban lifestyle with scads of leisure time for sitting at sidewalk
cafés, practicing yoga, musing, romping with pals, and occasionally
thinking deep thoughts in a windblown field. The trouble is, if all
these scenes are *too* real, the consumer might begin to think that
it doesn't matter what jeans you wear while you're being real. If
viewers just yearn for the reality of this young woman's life and
neglect to notice the jeans she's wearing, the Levi's 900 Series could
fall into the great void of ill-defined denim. We might end up being
sold on the lifestyle and ignoring the product.

At a certain point, the "real" in advertising becomes generic,
which means "anonymous," in brand language. So the advertising
objective must be to make things real, but *distinctively* real. Which
means so enticing that people will feel uneasy with who they are
and will want to have just a little bit *more*.

But what happens when an advertiser uses *real* people, not just
models or actresses *looking* real?

Now we have an added twist, and an intriguing one. What a "real person" ad promises is not just a new look, but the look of an estimable person who actually uses the advertiser's product or wears the advertiser's garment every day. This is the Barneys tack.

Barneys New York is a clothier that promotes an unequivocally upscale image of the kind of real men who dress up in Barneys finely tailored suits.

Here's a well-preserved, mature man, standing stiffly upright on a small, slightly elevated platform, hands clasped behind his back, sporting an elegant brown suit ensemble and an impassive expression. Above his head are the words "No Dummies." Now,

while it is obvious that this is not a photo of a store mannequin, it does appear to be a shot of a man who is presenting a fairly convincing facsimile of one. But the advertiser wants its audience to understand, as the bold copy of the ad elaborates, that "We know our customers have real bodies and tend to be active . . ."

This ad is part of a campaign in which Barneys uses New York personalities, rather than hired models, to display its wares. The rather stilted-looking gentleman chosen for this piece is, we learn at the end of the body copy, one Herb Schmertz, Wall Street financial consultant. For its very knowing audience in the greater New York area, Barneys expresses a very knowing perception of what "real . . . active" bodies look like by using a photograph of a mover-and-shaker who is calm on the surface and, presumably, a two-fisted hellion when he moves in for the day's action on Wall Street. Just as a person's appreciation of reality is always filtered through his or her *perceptions* of reality, Barneys' portrayal of its consumer's reality in this ad is transformed by the advertiser's perceptions. In this case, Barneys' perceptions of how an active, real person behaves is reflected in an image that looks more like a store mannequin than a living person. But the consumer audience knows what's up. Herb Schmertz is an actual guy, and the suit is part of what makes him dangerously effective as a mover-and-shaker.

Again, an advertiser is having a field day with our perceptions. "Schmertz is something that I'm not" is the implicit statement. And the most striking differences between Schmertz and all of us who aren't Schmertz is, as Barneys suggested, that suit. We know the suit is only part of the answer to the secret to Schmertz's business acumen, but we also know that people *do* dress for success, and so should we. With the New York celebrity campaign, Barneys offers its male consumers a suit that promises to take them to a more prosperous level of reality than ever before.

And all the men who are looking for professional success as well as personal identity look long and hard at Schmertz. What he's got, Barneys believes, men want. All of it.

Levels beyond levels. The ad game isn't called a game for nothing. And in this game, it is inevitable that the reality-chase continues until, eventually, a product catches itself looking at itself and asking, "Who am I, really?" Leave it to the magazine of the sixties (more fully alive than ever in the eighties) to perform such a feat of self-perception and self-identification in a dazzling campaign to upwardly mobilize its image with advertisers.

Rolling Stone magazine, in a much-ballyhooed, much-awarded campaign, has been playing an ad game with perception and reality since 1984—and with impressive results. The campaign is aimed squarely at the trade, meaning that the ads are meant to be read by media buyers in every consumer industry, from cereals, CDs, and motorcycles to cameras, cigarettes, and candy.

Rolling Stone hired Fallon McElligott, an agency known for its innovative, sometimes controversial creative work, to come up with a campaign that is deceptively simple: It uses contrasting images to illustrate the difference between advertisers' outdated "perceptions" of the twenty-one-year-old magazine's early readers (hippie dropout acid-rock fans) and the "reality," *today's* readers (hardworking heavy spenders with Volvos and credit cards to spare). McElligott's genius was in putting its finger on what potential advertisers perceived as the *Stone* reader's product preference, and then mounting an argument to counter that perception. Throughout the campaign, products themselves are the "visual language" that illustrate the distinction between perception and reality.

Consider this recent ad from the *Rolling Stone* campaign. The picture of the plastic bag of hand-dipped granola on the left side is headlined "Perception." On the side labeled "Reality" is a box of Post Grape-Nuts, under which is some body copy written to

Perception.

Reality.

For a new generation of Rolling Stone readers, breakfast comes from places like The A&P instead of the bulk bin at Alfalfa's Co-op. Last year, Rolling Stone readers crunched through more than 38 million servings of ready-made breakfast cereal. And the total bill at grocery store checkouts exceeded $18 billion. If you're looking for healthy appetites, you're invited to breakfast, lunch and dinner in the pages of Rolling Stone.

RollingStone

persuade advertisers that *Rolling Stone* readers shop at places where they spend money ("exceeded $18 billion") on name-brand products rather than grabbing gorp from "the bulk bin at Alfalfa's Co-op." If convinced, media buyers would abruptly realize that the *Rolling Stone* audience no longer fits the image of a bunch of back-to-nature freaks, but is a perfectly sensible market mature enough to buy its breakfast grains in portion-controlled form from a respectable company.

Ads like this, supported by the dauntless efforts of *Stone*'s assiduous sales force, have helped transform the magazine's image and have filled its pages with advertising gold. The "Perception/Reality" campaign has convinced hundreds of advertisers that the magazine has matured along with the flower children it nurtured and is now selling them the kinds of consumer goods that they used to spurn. In other words, *Rolling Stone* has accomplished the difficult task of convincing advertisers that readers have changed their personalities, tastes, and lifestyles even while faithfully renewing their subscriptions to that blast-from-the-past, *Rolling Stone.*

From a marketing viewpoint, *Rolling Stone* has tackled one of the most difficult problems in the arena of media buying—how to change advertisers' perceptions of a magazine that media buyers think they already know. The *perception* of the product (*Rolling Stone,* sixties style) had to be imagistically transformed into a new perception of the same-but-somewhat-altered product, which could then be labeled the new reality (*Rolling Stone,* eighties style).

Looking at the execution of *Stone*'s "Grape-Nuts" ad, I wondered how, of all the name-brand breakfast cereals lining supermarket shelves, *Rolling Stone* chose Post Grape-Nuts to represent the reality of its aging audience as well as its younger readers. I even wondered whether *Rolling Stone* had some deal going with Post.

Not at all, according to Les Zeifman, vice-president and associate publisher of *Rolling Stone.* "Grape-Nuts represents a healthy nutty product of the eighties," he said for the record.

Yes, I responded, but so do many others. There are numerous products that look just as natural as Grape-Nuts. So why choose the Post product to represent *Rolling Stone*'s reality?

Although Zeifman admitted to being just outside *Stone*'s eighteen- to thirty-four-year-old demographic, he divulged, "If you look in my cupboard, you'll find Grape-Nuts."

In other words, Mr. Zeifman, confessed Grape-Nuts customer, *perceived* that brand as symbolizing the *reality* of the new *Rolling Stone*'s readership because he eats the product and perceives himself as being a pretty typical reader.

He also agreed that his perceptions of the cereal could have been influenced by the brand's commercials. The *Rolling Stone* audience doesn't necessarily buy Grape-Nuts, but it was easy for Mr. Zeifman to construe that this audience would *probably* buy Grape-Nuts if they bought any boxed cereal.

Why?

Well, apart from the "Nature Poster" offering on the side of the box, just look at Grape-Nuts' advertising. Essentially, the Grape-Nuts' spots feature *thirtysomething* types wearing jeans and plaid flannel shirts in woodsy settings crunching their bowls of cereal in the great outdoors while drinking in the wholesomeness of it all. Clearly, these are people who have distanced themselves from the fringe origins of organic foods and have the money to enjoy their nature experiences in a vacation cottage. But, though their dollars go into the upscale, prepackaged Post product, their hearts still go for things natural, which fits with *Rolling Stone*'s publisher's perception of *Rolling Stone*'s audience. These *images* feed *Rolling Stone*'s *perceptions* of Grape-Nuts as symbolic of the branded breakfasts its *real* audience now buys.

What about the part of *Rolling Stone*'s audience that sees itself reflected on the "perception" side of the advertising equation? How do these people feel about *Rolling Stone*'s refurbished definition of its reality? They don't like it. To many of these older, long-term readers, the sixties are very much alive, and they see a *Rolling Stone* that has sold out.

Marsha, my friend and colleague, was one of the dropouts from the "new" *Rolling Stone*. She's in her late thirties, and was a devotee of *Rolling Stone* because of its liberal perspective. Marsha remembers precisely when she stopped buying the magazine. She tells me, "I was reading along and I saw this Marlboro ad, and it really turned me off. I probably acted too quickly, but all I could think was that *Rolling Stone* had copped out, and that was the end."

When a reader like Marsha becomes aware that the reality of *Rolling Stone* is no longer reflecting her perception of both the magazine and *of herself*, she registers her no-confidence vote the only way she can, by dumping her subscription. The readers who stayed with *Rolling Stone* were more moderate in their views and more open to the realities of consumerism; while younger subscribers are necessarily further away from the original heritage of *Rolling Stone*. To some extent, the change in *Rolling Stone*'s market was brought about by advertising shaping perceptions and by perceptions shaping reality—a two-way street.

There is one more layer of the dynamics between perception and reality to look at in *Rolling Stone*'s compaign: how advertisers perceive their selection as "perception" (past) and "reality" (present) in the different advertising executions. While advertisers' reactions to being positioned on the side of reality have been generally quite positive, *Rolling Stone* has occasionally misconstrued a product's current status as a counterculture item ("Perception") instead of an upscale consumer item ("Reality"). One such tiff occurred when a massive Harley-Davidson bike was labeled "Perception" at the same time the company—now a major *Rolling Stone* advertiser—was busy launching major licensing and advertising efforts targeted to moneyed members of the "Reality" market. The label inadvertently suggested that Harley-Davidson was not a "real" part of upscale lives.

Perception.

Another murmur of discontent was heard when a premium-priced imported beer was used as an example of the "Reality" of *Rolling Stone*'s market and was contrasted with an unlabeled keg —the keg of times gone by. The problem? This particular beer company objected to being *perceived* as fitting in with the other brands on the "Reality" side. It had no interest in joining *Rolling Stone*'s club of consumer "reality."

While much of advertising toys with our concepts of reality for dollars alone, the game takes on added seriousness when it gets us guessing about personal values and perceptions. This is expertly done, for instance, in an ad by Arian, Lowe & Travis, Inc., that was created for the Council for Retarded Citizens.

Unlike the ad-makers of *Rolling Stone*, the Council of Retarded Citizens isn't trying to lure new customers to a product; instead, it wants to encourage people to question their assumptions about retarded people. The Arian, Lowe & Travis message is deftly presented. And it's done by playing a variation of advertising's enigmatic reality game.

In the Arian, Lowe & Travis ad, two young men are sitting side by side as if posing for a portrait. Both wear glasses, both look directly at the audience, both are neatly groomed. One wears a suit and tie over his solid build; the other is smaller and wears a sport shirt and slacks on his thin, almost frail frame. As if we were watching a rerun of the old TV show *What's My Line,* the headline requests, "Will the real retarded person please stand up." Lee St. James, the agency's creative director, told me, "I wanted to make it sound like a command, like it did on *What's My Line.* so there's no question mark."

Unlike a game show, where getting the right answer is all that matters, here the winners are those who realize that the "correct" choice isn't so easy to guess after all. If we say it's the young man in casual attire, aren't we just making the easy mistake of assuming that the better-dressed person is inevitably the nonretarded person? On the other hand, we might try to outguess the advertiser (who just might be trying to fool us!) and say, "Well, I'm supposed to guess it's the skinny guy in shirtsleeves, so the correct answer *must be* the guy in the suit."

But wait a minute: Doesn't the guy in shirtsleeves "look" more retarded than the guy in the suit? Wait again: If we say that, what do we mean by "looks retarded"?

At this point, the guessing game turns on ourselves, which is exactly what the advertiser is trying to do. When do we label

Will the real retarded person please stand up.

Council for Retarded Citizens

someone as retarded? At first sight? When that person speaks? Are we prejudging people just by what they wear and how they look? And if so, how do our preconceptions of that person make us treat him differently? Are we ready to leap to value judgments about people based solely on whether they wear suits, part their hair every morning, and sit up straight?

If we care to consider this ad another moment, and go to another level, an additional zinger awaits us. Perhaps *both* of the young men are retarded. Perhaps *neither* is. Perhaps one is retarded in some ways, the other in other ways. (What, after all, do we mean by retarded?)

There's no "correct answer." Nowhere in the body of the ad does the copy reveal who the "real" retarded person is.

If we let this ad go to work on us, we are inevitably left with questions *inside ourselves.* The ad heightens our awareness of our preconceived conclusions about what a "real retarded person" *is.* Complex—but then, the Council for Retarded Citizens is selling *questioning,* a *thinking* process, which is a far more complex product than jeans or ad pages in a magazine.

By not solving the riddle of who's the "real" one, the Council for Retarded Citizens campaign tries to teach people to consider the unflattering possibility that if they're not psychologically equipped to accept the retarded in terms of their own basic humanity, then they suffer from a kind of retardation themselves— emotional retardation. From this perspective, there is no single right answer to the ad's challenge.

When advertisers ask us to test the realness of their imagery, they play on our inherent need to constantly test out the reality of our world. It's a basic human survival strategy that begins with the child's earliest struggle to sort out the difference between fantasy and reality, and between what is trustworthy and what is not. That is the psychological substrate, but advertisers, offering themselves as the authors of reality, siphon some of their power from our urgency, in our increasingly high-strung, computerized, dehumanized, breathlessly faxed culture, to *feel* real, to *be* real and to *seem real to others.*

Nobody wants to be seen as a phony, even if, deep down, he's terrified that he is. Advertising's "service" to us, if we can call it that, is to be the grand palliative remedy for our personal doubts, offering consumers a fine array of real (worn-out-looking) clothes and real (strawberry-colored) foods, and real (bottled) draft beer to shore up our images of ourselves as real, genuine people. And the closer advertisers get to creating images of reality that coincide with people's *perceptions* of what reality looks like, the harder it is for consumers to *test* the reality of a message and dismiss it as advertising.

Increasingly, however, advertisers who play with our perceptions face a problem of skepticism. Baby boomers who have been raised watching TV commercials can spot a marketing plan coming at them a mile away. Our collective fingers are poised over the remote-control zapper, ready to swiftly delete the blatant, the boring, the hyperbolic, the insulting. To counteract this impulse, television advertisers, especially, have begun to reach for a "new" level of reality represented by documentary film. These commercials are what I call docu-mercials. And they're proliferating with abandon.

But what makes something that *isn't* a documentary *look* like a documentary? Ironically, it's that most primitive and authentic of all the documentary filmmaker's tools, the hand-held camera!

So advertisers like AT&T and Honda Scooters decided that *jumpiness* in cinematography is a salient—*the* salient—cue to the "reality" of a filmed event for their target market. Ostensibly, these and other advertisers have shot their docu-mercials with hand-held cameras jiggly enough to induce a sense of motion sickness in the viewer. The look of genuine 33-millimeter home movies represents the "look" of a bygone era, and advertisers want to capitalize on this reminder of simpler times in the exponentially busier lives of the grown-up children who watched themselves in black-and-white moving pictures back in the fifties with Mom and Dad.

Docu-mercials are meant to be disarming. They are designed to reflect what advertisers hope are their buying market's perceptions of noncommercial *people* and noncommercial *film* as being unglamorous, fumbly, and grainy. Typically, the name of the product appears at the end of a series of vignettes, as if it were an afterthought, and as if the commercial weren't trying to sell anything at all. This breed of creative persuasion tries to slip past our advertiser-warning systems by pretending to be an engaging bit of reality rather than a commercial intruder.

Some slip by in their documentary-style guises: Advertisers call them successful. But others, trying the same ruse, set off the alarms and end up being zapped or even pilloried.

The American Telephone & Telegraph Company's commercials for its Business Markets Group were shot by a practicing documentary filmmaker, John Nathan, who was hired specifically by the company in order to give the spots a real-life aura. AT&T's is one of the docu-mercial campaigns that slipped by and landed on the side of the fence labeled marketing success. What success means, in this case, is that in the first six months the campaign ran, calls from businesses interested in the custom-made corporate phone systems, which can cost over $1 million, were up 250 percent.

The commercials feature a corporate supervisor who has obviously purchased a rotten phone system for his company. The miserable wretch is being chewed out by his superior; for a short time, we are treated to the spectacle of very unfunny close-ups of squirming anxiety. It's a classic egg-on-the-face experience, recorded with sufficient verisimilitude to make any viewer queasy.

According to AT&T's supervisor, William J. Higgins, the purpose of the spots was to show consumers "a world of angst, with the threat of failure." In the world of business communications, the corporate type who makes the wrong decision is in real peril. What if he installs a phone system that AT&T has already made obsolete? It could be a multimillion-dollar mistake.

The message came through loud and clear. The little vignettes resonate with real fear, and the target audience feels the kick in its solar plexus.

Small wonder that the phone calls increased by 250 percent. The misery portrayed in those commercials was only too vivid.

On the other hand, docu-mercials that *don't* seem real can be a major mistake, as with Chiat/Day's initial docu-mercials for Nissan Motors. The agency dramatized a group of Nissan engineers discussing the importance of designing humanistic cars. Judging from the documentary  quality of the filmmaking, we viewers were obviously supposed to believe that we were "right there," on the scene, inside an actual Nissan engineering office, overhearing an intense, eager group of engineers discuss the relative merits of certain "humanistic" features that can be found in new Nissans. These scenes were punctuated with quick cuts (courtesy of the shaky-camera technique) of real people doing real things with their Nissans . . . like lying on their hoods.

The trouble was, none of it rang true. The engineers' talk sounded forced and fabricated. No viewers with any consumer savvy believed for an instant that they were glimpsing the inside of an actual Nissan think tank. As for people lounging around on the hoods of their Nissans—is *this* supposed to look like the real thing? It was a sheer waste of good grainy docu-film.

Of course, the whole commercial was no farther from reality than any other commercial, but I believe it was the affectation of reality that killed it for good. It was just too much to take. Even the advertising industry was ready to pounce on this one. The Nissan docu-mercial became, almost instantly, one of the most talked-about bombs of the year. (The fact that Chiat/Day, creator of Apple's famed "1984" commercial, had come up with this loser was a particular source of delight to ad pundits. *Adweek* gave Nissan's "Engineers" spot its "Grand Baddie" award for having attained new heights of "phoniness.")

To make matters worse with consumers, the characters playing Nissan's engineer/designers in the spot were widely repudiated as being "yuppies." And their obvious smug self-satisfaction alienated precisely the target group that the commercial was meant to attract.

But Chiat/Day had no intention of creating a yuppie commercial. As Joe Opre, Nissan's national advertising manager, put it, "The agency wanted to do advertising that didn't look like advertising." So how did it come off looking so fake? Maybe the actors were just trying too hard to look real. The agency took pains to inject reality into the script; after all, the "conversations" the "engineers" have are all based on real, taped conversations with actual Nissan engineers.

But there's a huge chasm between the unpolished meanderings of human communication and the edited form that the agency used in its script. As it comes across in the commercial, the "natural" dialogue consists of nothing more than a number of *bon mots* that capsulize Nissan's tag line—"Built for the Human Race." Words sound unctuous rather than authentic. The actors represent mass-marketable Caucasians as well as minority groups: It's obvious to the viewer that all the "real" engineers were preselected by central casting. The result isn't just a credibility gap, it's a credibility canyon, and I believe it happened not just because the actors in "Engineers" are so stereotypically yuppified. I believe the spot turned people off because it puffed itself up as real, as a documentary, insider view of the thinking and thinkers behind Nissan, but came across as staged. It made people angry because it looked as if the advertiser thought the audience was a bunch of dupes. People already feel that yuppie culture and artifacts are fraudulent; when actual Nissan engineers are played by actors who are earnestly portraying stereotypes of sincere humans doing their best to make mankind more automotively comfortable, the phoniness quotient shoots off the charts. Cynics had a heyday with this one. Predictably, the Chiat/Day Nissan commercial inspired one very funny parody.

Music Television (MTV) was so tickled by Nissan's "Engineers" that it produced a send-up of the spot as a promotional piece for its station called *Nissan My Children*. The spoof (produced and directed by Barbara Kanowitz) is cast with a similar representation of minorities, including an Oriental who scoops up rice with chopsticks while all the other "engineers" sit around the same big table taking themselves seriously. The guy who kicks off the discussion has the same portly build and trendy red suspenders as in the original spot, only here, he devours doughnuts from a huge mound in front of him. With meaningful emphases, the group ponders the kind of channel it wants MTV to be: "People want *more* . . . they want to *belong* . . . But it's gotta be *spontaneous* and it's gotta be *unpredictable*—and folks, that takes *planning*." The spot concludes with the doughnut-gobbler commenting sardonically on the central failing in the original spot: "Why are we sitting around here talking like this? *We* don't work for MTV."

Even Lee Clow, Chiat/Day's president and executive director, admits, when he considers the reviews of the agency's Nissan commercial, "If we made a mistake, it was not using the real engineers."

What about Chiat/Day's latest spots for Nissan? They're docu-mercials again. But this time around, real Nissan owners are snuggling up to their cars. Because the owners are not pretending not to be pretending, the docu-mercials ring true emotionally, even though we know they're commercials.

So much for reality.

However, advertising also has other masters to serve, and among those masters are the politicians who seek to present a "real message" to the electorate. With televisions in 98 percent of American homes, the advertising world has now taken on the momentous task of delivering, in fifteen- to thirty-second doses, powerful messages about those whom we are supposed to elect to the presidential office. But whereas agencies can have fun putting together a commercial for cars, cereal, or detergent, it gets tougher—and sometimes messier—when they have to cram a conceptual message rather than a consumer plea into a television-commercial spot. And particularly when that message has to deal with such big issues as health, wealth, defense, and world peace.

All *that* in thirty seconds?

Obviously, we're going to get overload. And overload is just what we got in '88 between Bush and Dukakis. But the '88 commercials, though perhaps more dreadful in some ways than anything that came before, were not without precedent.

The '88 campaign may well have been the first election during which more analysis was devoted to the candidates' commercials than to the candidates themselves. Why? The imagery turned out to be more electrifying than the candidates. The transformation of a George Bush from being relegated to an asterisk in a *Doonesbury* cartoon to being a stand-up-kind-of-war-hero, and of a Mike Dukakis from steady budget-balancer from Massachusetts to grinning tank commander—these turned out to be the stories of how people perceive the candidates rather than stories about the candidates themselves. And the news media, needing to fill a vacuum with *some* news about the candidates, played along beautifully by reviewing, commenting on, and in some cases even rerunning (on unpaid airtime!) the missiles that the candidates launched against each other.

On the street, at cocktail parties, and in focus groups, people tended to voice their predictable revulsion to negative political advertising. But I believe this revulsion reflects a deeper skepticism toward the media in general. Having lived through the lies of Vietnam, Watergate, and the Iran-Contra affair—not to mention the dirty laundry of local politics—people assume at this point that they're better off with a cynical view of the entire process.

That way, they won't be caught looking naive. To preserve its own honor, the public takes negative, distorting political campaigns as a given, and has little faith in the illusion that it will ever be able to know candidates as "real people."

What is the evidence for this disillusionment? It is nearly impossible to isolate and identify the impact of paid ads over other factors such as the debates (if you can call predigested formulas spewing from candidates in carefully monitored alternating mouthfuls "debates"), direct mail, "truth squads" (politicians assigned by each side to refute what the opponents' ads were saying), media coverage, and "spin doctors" attempting to sway journalists' reports in favor of their candidates. But one unusual event, one simple statistic, is revealing: The 1988 presidential election had the lowest voter turnout in sixty-four years. Yes, both candidates were less than charismatic; yes, the campaign was long and tiresome. But when it comes right down to it, maybe the American public recoiled from the transparent trivialization of democracy. After all, who wants to exercise his right to vote for a commercial?

Abstention would be harmless enough if we were simply abstaining from the purchase of cola, beer, or cereal. But the political process *should* be more important, somehow, than the cola wars. Much of the media attention given to the handling of the candidates raised deeper concerns about the way the political process is heading. Is it *really* okay to peddle presidents like soft drinks?

Obviously, it isn't quite okay. We want more. The candidates' promoters know that. And one of their best tactics is to play upon our more serious concerns about the people we're electing—sometimes with great effectiveness.

If there's one theme that recurs again and again in presidential-candidate commercials, it's the theme of dread. Put bluntly, we fear what these candidates (whom we never, ever know very well) can do to us. The candidate who can fill the electorate with the most dread of the other—and a dread of what that candidate can do—is the man who probably stands the best chance of winning.

It's a new tack on the reality issue. But instead of trying to get across the "real" candidate in thirty seconds or less, advertisers go for a quick snapshot of the "reality" of the threatening world we all live in.

Enter Willie Horton.

When I saw the media momentum and public concern generated by Bush's focus on Willie, a convicted murderer who, having escaped while on a weekend pass from Dukakis's Massachusetts prison-furlough program, managed to commit rape and assault, I thought about what Willie Horton symbolizes. His significance clearly went deeper than that of the specter of crime conjured by his menacing photo in the papers. It wasn't just Horton who was terrifying. Bush's "Revolving Door" spot, created by Frankenberry, Laughlin & Constable/Milwaukee, shot in the sobering shadows of black-and-white film, showed silhouetted prison guards helpless to stem the flow of inmates out the "revolving door" of the Massachusetts prison-furlough program. It was this image of unchecked aggressive impulses that tapped into people's fears. And Willie Horton became the symbol for what would get out if Dukakis got in.

Now where does "reality" fit into the revolving-door ad, or should we ask, how does the revolving-door image fit into reality?

The bleak prison scene featuring the watchtower and the strolling guard are real enough to remind us of a netherworld of criminality just beyond our collective doorstep. The scenes strongly suggest that only high walls and barbed-wire security prevent the forces of lawlessness and disorder from being unleashed. While the "revolving door" scenes are staged, the convicts look sufficiently thuggish to make us thoroughly uneasy about meeting them in a dark alley. Given the juxtaposition of the revolving door with real guards and real walls, the symbols of an easy come, easy go prison system are dramatically effective. The message: Dark Forces will stroll out, should Mike Dukakis be elected.

Media watchers fretted and fumed while they debated this one. Those on Dukakis's side deplored the way the emotion-grabbing visuals misrepresented his political views and legislative actions. Those on the Bush side stood by the "statement" of the "Revolving Door" campaign: Deep down, they argued, the Duke really didn't care about protecting America from its Willie Hortons. And then there were others who merely stood aghast at the whole campaign, who were disgusted with the way the spot played on the gullibility of the American public and conveyed the cynicism of the makers of America's commercials.

But I think something else went on during the "Revolving Door" campaign—something that may in fact bring all of us (voters, media watchers, partisan politicians, bemused bystanders) closer to the reality issue than we necessarily want to be. Viewing the Willie Horton campaign and its suggestions of Dark Forces, I was distinctly reminded of another, more powerful Dark Forces commercial that ran for a short, indelible moment in 1964.

In the 1964 presidential battle between Lyndon Johnson and Barry Goldwater, Johnson ran a cataclysmic commercial, "Daisy/Girl/Peace," which stirred up alarming emotions and shaped profound fears that Goldwater was a hawk of the lunatic kind, ready to nuke the Communists into oblivion at the slightest provocation. In the spot, pictures of a little girl plucking the petals off a daisy, in a mind-bending countdown metaphor, were interspersed with the growing mushroom cloud of a nuclear explosion.

The emotional power of that commercial was staggering. I didn't realize it at the time, but the commercial aired only once. Psychologically, the spot pushed all the right buttons. It unearthed the horror of devastating destruction that could be wrought by the Oval Office occupant and it symbolized the same terrifying loss of control as Willie Horton did.

At the very least, a leader in this country is supposed to be

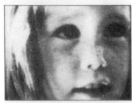

able to keep order with a cool head—to keep feelings from getting out of hand, to ensure that reason prevails over primitive impulses in society—in short, to be able to play a mature, quasiparental role. What "Revolving Door"and "Daisy/Girl/Peace" symbolize takes advantage of our deep-seated anxiety about our own dependency on such a leader. These spots heighten our sense of vulnerability and provoke fears about the unknown and unpredictable character of the next president (whoever he is). Will murderers and rapists walk freely among us? Will nuclear Armageddon be unleashed?

Critics of such emotionally ripping material see these commercials as extreme and alarmist. And they are. But they also get to the root of our anxieties about our society, our security, and our future. Interestingly enough, if you take away the names of the candidates, what you are left with are symbolic representations of two extraordinarily important issues, the disastrous condition of the criminal justice system and the horrific power of our nation's nuclear arsenal.

Yet another example of the "reality" issue in politics was Reagan's campaign in 1984. Not surprisingly, the Dark Force represented in *that* campaign was communism.

For Reagan's message, the candidate's admen, the Tuesday Team, seized upon the figure of a dark, rambling, silently menacing bear as the symbol of prowling communism. The team tapped into powerful stuff. In terms of psychology

PRESIDENT REAGAN

PAID FOR BY REAGAN-BUSH '84

and ancient mythology, the bear symbolizes the most basic, instinctual, and dangerous layers of the unconscious: fear and aggression that must be controlled for the good of society.

In the Reagan "Bear" spot, no candidate is shown. Instead, we saw a huge bear prowling its natural habitat and heard this voice-over: "There is a bear in the woods. For some people, the bear is easy to see. Others don't see it at all. Some people say the bear is tame. Others say it's vicious and dangerous. Since no one can really be sure who's right, isn't it smart to be as strong as the bear? If there is a bear?"

In the Reagan commercial, again we have a very "real" issue played out in evocative symbolic terms for a political purpose. The "threat of communism" is a preoccupation that has consumed the American electorate, and has, to a large degree, determined the rise and fall of candidates' political fortunes since the end of World War II. In drawing the fearsome bear from the woods and putting him, at full prowl, on home viewing screens, the Tuesday Team brought the electorate into direct confrontation with an issue that has lurked behind every foreign policy, disarmament, and defense decision for the past four decades.

On one level, the bear symbolizes Russia and the need for Reagan's advocacy of a strong defense.

But the psychological significance, and effectiveness, of the "Bear" spot goes deeper, and shares the symbolic meaning of a Willie Horton or a nuclear explosion. The psychological messages cutting across the winning images of a nuclear explosion, or a bear, or a Willie Horton taps into our innermost terror of being annihilated by the outbreak of violent, irrational Dark Forces, and offers a Johnson or a Reagan or a Bush as the antidote to these fears.

But despite the *real* Dark Forces issues that have lurked around every recent political campaign, trivialization finally wins out, perhaps because the darker issues themselves are too troublesome to confront.

So, in the final desperate days of the Dukakis campaign, the American electorate was treated to the ultimate (let us hope) redundancy of a presidential-packaging campaign. Dukakis's counterattack to the Bush "Revolving Door" spot was a series of commercials called "The Packaging of George Bush," produced for Dukakis by the Sawyer/Miller Group. In this series, Dukakis attempted to denigrate his opponent by showing Bush's "advisers" (they were all actors) conferring about how to distort Dukakis's record and how to script Bush for success. One spot focuses on four behind-the-scenes "strategists" disparaging Bush as the candidate who, rather than counter an issue, "wraps himself up in the American flag," and closes with, "They'd like to sell you a package. Wouldn't you rather choose a president?"

Like Nissan's unfortunate "Engineers" spot, "The Packaging of George Bush" sought to hook the public with a docu-mercial peek into the inner workings of the minds behind the construct, while protesting that the fabrication was real. The Dukakis series backfired because it didn't just ask the public to believe that a commercial wasn't really a commercial, it asked the public to believe that the guy who hired a bunch of actors to portray sleazy presidential packagers wasn't a packager *himself*. And with a bunch of knowing cynics like the American electorate, that ploy wouldn't even pass the scrutiny of a twelve-year-old.

In "Packaging," Dukakis's packagers hoped to differentiate him as "real" from Bush as "packaged," but televised political advertising has been around since Eisenhower first used it in his 1952 election. It's no news to Americans that political advertising tries

to manipulate their perceptions of the candidate. A candidate who self-righteously declares himself to be above using images to shape public opinion, while turning out commercials packaging his opponent as being packaged, comes across as a hypocrite.

But it may be revealing to contrast the intellectual failure of commercials like "Packaging" with the purely visceral, emotion-packed success of the revolving door, the mushroom cloud, and the prowling bear. In "Packaging," we're looking at the docudrama that fails to document anything because it's trying so hard to look real that it only succeeds in looking fake. In the successful Dark Forces commercials, on the other hand, images are used for clearly symbolic messages. Those messages do get at real issues—crime, nuclear war, communism—in representational terms that make the best use of advertising's high-intensity visual shortcuts.

But what's being "sold" in these emotion-packed, pseudopolitical messages? We're not being sold a party platform, or a set of priorities, or even much of a reason to vote for (or against) a candidate. We're certainly not being asked to make intellectual choices on issues such as innovations to the criminal-justice system, or a new disarmament policy, or an overhaul of our foreign relations. The ad agencies and advisers aren't fooled and they aren't fooling us: They know that the candidates they represent have no startling policy changes in mind for America, and they know that a "true" representation of new political ideas would simply be a blank screen.

But these commercials are very good at showing us what we fear the most. Advertising teams may or may not know what Americans love about America, but they are lucid about what is most troubling to Americans—and that's what ends up on the screen. The ad teams know that if we *believe* we can tame the Dark Forces at the polls by voting in a fearless leader, we'll probably try.

The trouble is, if we *don't* believe we can do anything about those forces, and can't separate a candidate from his construct, we'll probably stay home. Which is what happened in 1988.

CHAPTER 7

SEX, SIN, AND SUGGESTION

She struts into my office wearing one of her favorite looks, a tight dress and high black boots. As she folds her lanky thirty-year-old body into a chair, she automatically arranges her massive auburn hair so it falls over one shoulder, tilts her head coquettishly, and begins to tell me what's on her mind.

Marlene is a receptionist in a small publishing company and has been married for two years. She and Tom had fallen madly in love and had had an active sex life all through the first year of their marriage, but then Marlene found herself less excited by Tom, less passionate about making love as frequently—less interested. Marlene was beginning to worry that something was seriously wrong with her, and with her ability to love.

I asked Marlene what she thinks she *ought* to be feeling, and she stops looking coquettish and starts looking nervous. "I know I look hot," she says. "Well, I *ought* to *feel* as hot as I *look*. It's not that Tom doesn't turn me on anymore—he does. It's just that I don't want it all the time like I used to when we first got together.

All those young things out there—and I know Tom looks at them—I'm scared he's going to start running around because I'm not lusting after him all the time like I used to. And then I go out and buy something hot to wear to make myself feel sexier. Tom always tells me how great it is with me, but I don't know whether to believe him. It doesn't even matter—I'm the one who's upset. I feel like I've lost something."

I ask Marlene how she figures that after two years of marriage her sex life would be just as exciting as when she first fell in love. Marlene looks embarrassed and tentatively begins to tell me about her insecurities. When she was a teenager she thought she was ugly, that no boy would ever like her. She wanted to be beautiful and seductive. Then she tells me how she used *ads* directly, deliberately, to teach herself how to look sexy. She tells me she'd practice holding her lips in the open, pouty way models do when they sell makeup, or arching her back to push out her chest, or bending over to show off her rear like she saw in all the jeans ads. Secretly, Marlene wanted to be a model, and worked hard at learning the moves.

Marlene's grown older, but the images on the commercials haven't, and she's still measuring herself against them. She sees the young, flirtatious, sexy couples, and it's her and Tom all over again, except that she's not feeling exactly the same. The gap between the images and her reality has widened—a perfectly natural part of maturing relationships—but nothing matures in advertising's time warp. Marlene still *looks* like the same package—but she's no longer *living* the same package—and she feels the gap as a failure.

Marlene feels as if something is wrong with her because the normal ebb and flow of sexual intensity over time in a marriage falls completely outside her expectations of herself. Marlene says Tom is content with the level of their lovemaking, *and with her,* but Marlene isn't as comfortable or secure and tends to be more tied in to cultural pressures than to her own husband's reassurance. Why?

I look over at Marlene and I know she still can't believe that Tom fell in love with *her* and not her mannerisms, and she can't believe that she fell in love with Tom and wasn't just playacting. When the early rushes of sexual passion mellowed, she panicked.

She was terrified Tom would find out how empty and insecure she felt inside, and leave her.

It's no wonder Marlene still has strong feelings about sexy fantasies in advertising; they feed her search for how to act and who to be, in order to get love. And advertising constantly reminds her of how much she continues to try to create herself in the image of magazine models.

Sex *is* rampant in advertising. And no other type of psychological imagery hits people closer to where they really live. Advertisers didn't create the need for men and women to feel sexually viable, and advertisers didn't create the insecurities people have about being able to love. These are core issues in human development that cut right through to the heart of self-esteem, where people are most vulnerable. And advertisers, because they're in the business of making money, have long dangled the lure of enhanced sexuality to motivate consumers to buy.

Does sex in advertising sell? Sometimes.

Does sex in advertising attract attention? Yes. Does sex in advertising influence people? Yes. And vice versa.

Some of the most pervasive, and persuasive, sexual imagery in advertising is more symbolic than blatant, although the connotations are often far from subtle. The ad for Chanel lipstick by Doyle Dane Bernbach (Milan) shows a woman with her upturned, open mouth grasping a tube of the product between her teeth. The red lipstick is fully extended, her eyes are closed, and her face shows

pleasure. The image is visually arresting, clearly evocative of fellatio, and symbolically links the cosmetic with the promise of sexual allure.

What Chanel is selling here isn't simply lipstick; the imagery sends a message to the unconscious, granting permission to fulfill sexual wishes and points the way to an attractor that can facilitate the encounter. But she's also thumbing her nose—symbolically sticking her tongue out

Seagram's
Extra Dry

Gin

AMERICA'S No.1
SELLING GIN

—at conventional refinement. She's playful, arrogant, and Chanel uses that message (intentionally or not) as a way of poking fun at its own reserved image.

Seagram's Extra Dry Gin ad, created by Ogilvy & Mather, is on a direct line to the male unconscious with its imagery. Dominating the center of the page is a huge Spanish olive, its nearly neon-red pimiento pushing out at the viewer as it is engulfed by a clear, viscous liquid. Presumably, the fluid is Seagram's Extra Dry Gin, an elixir that, the headline claims, can "Arouse an Olive." Metaphorically speaking, this is a very sexy imperative and a very sexy product benefit. The archetypal shape, signifying the female, which has endured since the Paleolithic Era, is round. À la olive. And this one, with its bulging scarlet center, is suggestive both of a tumescent clitoris or nipple—and essentially of a woman in a state of arousal. The invitation "Arouse an Olive," written in a classic masculine typeface, is psychologically directed to men, and delivers a message that promises, and then visually delivers, a sexual seduction, complete with a climactic outpouring of liquid.

Psychological analysis aside, it's gut-level obvious what the advertiser's up to here. "Arouse" is not a word generally applied to an olive.

The sexual message Seagram's Extra Dry Gin symbolizes in its "Olive" ad is sent, but more overtly, in a different ad for the same product. In the upper right is a picture of an upright bottle (male) overlapping the rounded edge of an orange (female)—a graphic echo of the lower-right image of a couple in heated embrace. As if there could be any doubt about the advertiser's imbuing Seagram's Gin with aphrodisiac powers, the copy reads like a litany of praises for the product's capabilities, which ends with the line, positioned as being spoken by the lovers, "They also say it could turn a 'maybe' into . . . 'again.' " Interpreted at its most basic level, the ad's message about the link between the product and sexuality would appear to be "Get her drunk and get her in bed."

It's easier for consumers to dismiss the transparent seduction of the "Maybe" Seagram's ad than the symbolic, indirect sexual message of the "Arouse" piece. Symbolic communications bypass the layers of logic and cultural appropriateness and head straight for the unconscious, which is then free to find an equivalence between what is symbolized, in this case sexual arousal, and the brand, Seagram's Extra Dry Gin.

Marlene's right. The pressures to be sexy, stay sexy, and get sexier are enormous. We are a driven culture, and the fuel firing the more-is-always-better machine is internal as well as external. Madison Avenue's *pressure* to measure up is only matched in intensity by the level of *need* to measure up that people bring to the relationship. And that need boils down to the need to love and be loved.

People who are secure enough to develop an enduring, mutual, affectionate relationship with another person have accomplished an extraordinarily difficult psychological task. Too often, people get stuck in their insecurities; in their desperate determination not to expose their insecurities, they frantically try to fill up a sense of emptiness with cultural facsimiles of love. And the culture—with advertisers ranking right up there, our sergeant-at-arms of imagery—holds up an endless array of tempting surrogates in designer packaging: popularity, prestige, glamour, sexiness.

What's vicious about this particular cycle is that the more people try to fill themselves up by propping up the *outside*, the more terrified they are about exposing who they really are on the *inside*. The discrepancy becomes too great, and the investment in the decoy self becomes too high to risk losing whatever security it does provide. Probably the single biggest barrier to love is the fear of psychological exposure, of being found out and found lacking.

When advertisers link products with sexuality, they lock in with people's deepest fears of being unlovable; they offer their products and images as the tickets to love, when what they're really providing are more masks for people to hide behind.

When I was about fourteen, my friend's aunt unwittingly provided me with a shocking revelation. Aunt Eva was always beautifully coiffed and painted and jeweled and cinched. When I was younger, I'd harbored the fantasy that she was a movie star. I remember standing in the bathroom with her while she was making up her eyes and asking how she got it all off when she went to sleep. Aunt Eva turned to me and whispered, as if she were giving me the greatest beauty secret of all, "I *don't* take it off—I just touch it up when I go to bed. I don't want Uncle George to see me without my face on!" I was stunned. It was one of those concepts that makes the world stop for an instant. Here was this gorgeous lady who had been married to the same man for twenty years or so, and she couldn't let him see her without makeup. At the time, I didn't understand why this revelation unnerved me so much, but I know I felt sorry for Uncle George and creepy about Aunt Eva. She was all surface.

Aunt Eva may not have felt very lovable as a person, and Uncle

George may have been the kind of guy who needed to see his woman always made up. I think of Aunt Eva now as someone who might describe herself as a list of physical attributes, as if she were placing an ad in the personal classifieds. And she might look for the same kinds of qualities in a man, so neither of them would have to get too close, or reveal too much.

Young & Rubicam's ad for R. J. Reynolds Tobacco Company's More cigarettes actually *uses* the device of a personal classified to position the product as capable of fulfilling the need for a relationship. And the nature of that relationship, as defined by the advertiser's imagery, has nothing to do with real intimacy. The emphasis is strictly superficial, strictly sexual, and strictly uncommitted.

In the More ad, the circled classified reads: "WANTED. Tall, dark stranger for long lasting relationship. Good looks, great taste a must. Signed, Eagerly Seeking Smoking Satisfaction." A brown More cigarette lies across a corner of the clipping—it's the "tall, dark stranger" himself. Headlined in red at the bottom is "Find More Pleasure." Yes, the quest is on, and this cigarette promises a fast track to heightened sexual experiences. Yes, the woman knows what she wants and she wants more of it, and what that looks like, from the advertising message, is to be able to use a man to satisfy her sexual demands—and nothing else. It's cigarette as stud; stud as dildo. The ad symbolizes a sexual encounter that carries no threat of exposure, no threat of anything getting too close for comfort. The "long lasting relationship" is with a "stranger," and it appears to be a consistent feature of More's image to put the woman in charge of keeping it that way.

In another More ad, the symbolic tryst between strangers is realized, and the sexual innuendoes of the personal classified become a seductive dialogue about foreplay. In this ad, the models are black, with the photos cropped so that only the lower halves of their faces are visible. Eye contact, with its associated potential

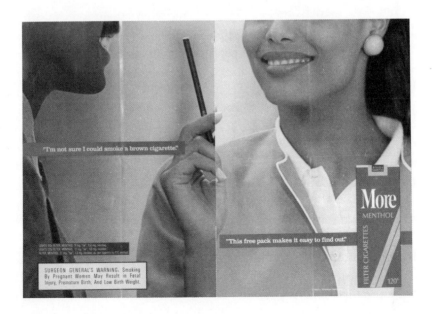

for emotional intimacy, has been eliminated as part of the communication. These two might as well be wearing masks. The man says to the woman holding a More cigarette, "I'm not sure I could smoke a brown cigarette."

Now, when would a man question his ability to smoke a cigarette because of its *color?* When he's not really talking about a cigarette at all. In this symbolic context, the question is a reference to sex, lightly tinged with racial overtones. Evidently, the woman possesses whatever special inclinations or talents are required in order to "smoke a brown cigarette," and tries to persuade him, Evelike, to see if he can manage it as well, as she says enticingly, "This free pack makes it easy to find out."

Within this framework, the woman is dominant, an image that is congruent with More's cigarlike coloration and accentuated length, and she appears confident about how to handle the "brown cigarette." On a deeper level, the man's doubts about smoking could reflect unconscious doubts about his own sexual identity, which casts a different light on his ambivalence about putting the "brown cigarette" in his mouth. Smoking More cigarettes is positioned as a very sexy thing for a woman to do, and the sexiness appears to be tied up with power—the power that a woman, perhaps even unsure of *her* sexual identity, might derive from being in control of a man.

Cheesy sexual-power games are recurrent themes in another long-standing cigarette campaign. Newport, a product of Lorillard, Inc., has been successfully profiting from associating cigarettes with themes of sexual dominance and submission for a decade. Targeted to a young market, the campaign's slogan is "Alive with pleasure!" What Newport's imagery suggests, in ad after ad, is that its smokers will become *sexually* alive with pleasure. The gist of the campaign is that if it feels good, do it, an insidiously shrewd strategy for a product that invites people to sell their birthrights to health for a bowl of momentary pleasure.

In one vivid example of the ravishing sexual adventures young singles *could* have if they started smoking Newports, two men are carrying a long pole between them from which is hanging, in deer-bounty fashion, their female prey. All three are having a great time as her head hangs down exactly at one man's crotch level, while her up-ended legs expose her rear to the opposite man—at just

about the right level for a soft-porn ménage à trois. Just as the primary acceptable justification today's smokers can feed themselves is simply that they *like* to smoke, sexual entanglements like the merry threesomes are justified as worthy of pursuit as long as they're fun. As Newport puts it in the ad's closing tag line, "After all, if smoking isn't a pleasure, why bother?"

There's nothing wrong with a fun fantasy, except that while the sexy scene can remain solely in consumers' imaginations, smoking and its medical sequelae are very real indeed. The advertiser's imagery isn't intended to get consumers to *fantasize* about Newports, it's designed to get consumers to *smoke* Newports. All the persuasive copy and visuals going into pushing the *pleasure* of Newports are just as busy pushing the pleasure of sexuality, a human drive that needs no advertising support. The unconscious doesn't separate the product from the passion, and sexual *expectations* get sold just as hard as the brand.

Men in this culture feel just as pressured to exude sexual prowess and proficiency as women, and advertisers provide steady, compelling reinforcement of these expectations. There is no dearth of ads offering men groaning boards heaped with tasty images of available young women, designed to whet their appetites for associated consumer goods. But does it work? Does sex sell?

Women perceive romantic imagery and even symbolic metaphors (like the Chanel ad) as sexy; to men, nudity means sexiness. While women can look at ads with considerable sexual content and still remember what brand is being promoted, when men are faced with overtly sexual imagery, they can't remember *anything*—often they can't even describe what was in the ad, let alone name the product! Sexy ads *do* rivet a man's attention, but the intellectual circuits can get overloaded fast and, at that point, all that gets marketed is food for fantasies. And that's no cause for a bottom-line celebration. If their consumer target can't ask for it by name, the advertiser has just squandered a bundle. For men in this culture trying to grow up, to move from sexual preoccupations into committed relationships, advertisers' sexual preoccupations help keep them stuck in the crippling quicksand of adolescence. And that's no cause for psychological celebration.

Danny is one guy who's working hard to make it as a faithful, loving husband. Despite a solid emotionally and physically satisfying relationship with his wife, he feels confused and troubled by sexual fantasies. At thirty-five, and after ten years of marriage, Danny thinks he should have grown out of his attraction to other women, and has a particularly trying time in the spring, alternating between guilt and glee when discarded coats reveal flimsy feminine fabrics and more. At this point, after a fairly intensive course of self-examination, Danny feels as though it's almost all right for him to gawk and imagine and otherwise indulge the benign oglings that appear to be an intrinsic part of the normal male sex drive. As long as he doesn't act out his fantasies, a breach that would be virtually unthinkable in his particular marriage, his wife can't see what all the fuss is about. But there's another side to this picture of Danny's furtive mental stimulation, and I catch a glimpse of it when I ask him if he thinks other men worry about how much they fantasize. Danny answers, "A lot of people I've known have cheated—so they're worried about getting caught, they've caved in to their impulses. And in a way, I'd start to worry about myself if I *didn't* get the urge. And then there's all those ads—everywhere you look, there's some girl looking hot to trot. Jesus, they're even hanging over me on billboards! And then I look at my wife—and she's beautiful and I love her—but she's had two kids, and I feel like I've known her all my life. It's easy to fantasize that your wife will always be twenty and glamorous, and that you'll always be seductive. It's a con job, really, because if you buy all the fantasies—if you start to go after it—you can drive yourself nuts. It can be like a drug."

So, it's not just that Danny feels guilty for looking or fantasizing; he feels that he's got to measure up to the expectations that get set up by the media. Advertisers play on his fantasies, and he's attracted to the sexy women they serve up for him, but then the line between reality and fantasy starts to blur and increases the pressure to live it out in real life. When Danny feels less sexually

Introducing Pierce's
Impeccably Sophisticated
Yet Refreshingly Casual
Cuervo Gold Sunset.

attracted to his wife than he does to a woman in an ad, he starts to lose faith in himself.

I have no idea whether Danny has ever seen Young & Rubicam's ad for Cuervo Tequila, but it is a tailor-made example of the kind of Don Juan imagery he is battling. The centerpiece of the ad is not the product—it's a tall, dark, handsome, velvet-suited and bow-tied rake, wearing a slightly debauched smirk. Fixing a bedroom leer at the reader, he holds the drink he has in one hand toward a blond woman looking up at him, while he pours a bottle of Cuervo Gold into the surreptitiously held glass of *another* woman gazing admiringly at him. Women in the background smile radiantly. Who is this mesmerizing fellow—this paragon of manhood? The copy tells us that what we are witnessing is "Impeccably Sophisticated Yet Refreshingly Casual Cuervo Gold." But it doesn't sound like a liquor. It sounds like a description of our suave hero and his sexual interludes. *He* is the product personality. *He* is where the action is. *He* is what's being sold. And even if it's broad, and even if it's obvious, it still goes into the mix—and the image adds its weight to the critical mass of sexual expectations that men face in this culture.

Cuervo Gold wants a man to identify with the particular charisma of a Don Juan; someone like Danny doesn't necessarily *want* to be a Don Juan. There may be a Continental *savoir-faire* to the Cuervo ad, but for the man who's less interested in Spanish intrigue and more interested in being seduced, there's Hennessy.

In Schieffolin & Somerset Company's ad for the Hennessy brand the advertiser casts the lure of a sultry, willing woman—*his* for the asking. Of course, first he'd have to imbibe the cognac that, as the tag line conveys, isn't a liquor at all—it's "The Spirit of the Civilized Rogue." It all looks so easy, so available. What a fantasy of sexual seduction! What a big-as-life close-up of tousled, eyes-only-for-you, full-lipped female come-hitherness! The Hen-

nessy ad is an entreaty to identify with—to measure up to—the image of being the kind of man who could summon this scene, and could elicit the irresistible invitation the woman extends: "You don't look comfortable in that tie."

Hennessy has long been promoted as "civilized," but while earlier ads showed scenes of seduction that the target consumers looked in on, such as a gentleman dropping over to an appreciative lady's apartment with his Hennessy and two glasses in hand ("The civilized way to open doors"), Hennessy's latest ad plunges the man into the immediacy of a face-to-face encounter with the spoils of a rogue's life, albeit a "civilized rogue."

There's a lot going on here. The cognac is upscale. So the ad has to convey refinement, expensive tastes (Hennessy isn't cheap), mellow fireglow, and the leisure of the "civilized rogue," while the *woman* conveys a straightforward come-on. This is all accomplished with flowing hair, superb indirect lighting, and the kind of perfect manicure that a very elegant rogue's very cultivated companion would never go without. Compared to the Cuervo Gold ad, this is life in the slow lane; but it's a slow lane filled with limousines, chateaux, candlelight, and lion pelts by the fire.

Liquor ads have to work hard, because they're justifying their price with their image. At face value, what they're selling is inebriation, and all that that connotes. But certainly more than alcohol content is being promoted. What liquor advertisers have going for them is a long history of sexual experiences induced, allowed, or enhanced by alcohol. The sexual image conjures those experiences. And the precise evocation of that sexual image positions that product in the beholder's eyes. But then, that's what brand personality is all about. Without this kind of scenic, psychological embellishment, what is Hennessy but just another 80 proof cognac?

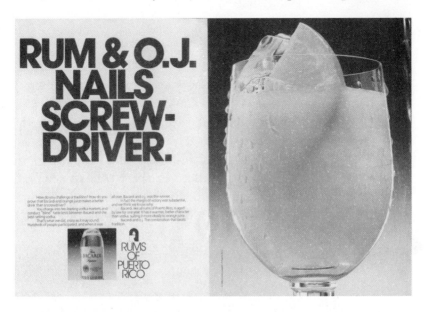

Even when it's not trying to, liquor advertising can't seem to do much else but ride on sexuality's mileage. A splendidly tacky example of how far an advertiser is willing to travel in this same direction comes our way in the form of Commonwealth of Puerto Rico's promotional piece for the rums of Puerto Rico. On the right-hand side, a luscious shot glass of orange juice; on the left, the boldfaced words "Rum & O.J. Nails Screwdriver." This stuff is just about on a par with the graffiti found in high school bathrooms. I suppose it grabs attention. Negative attention. And the macho sexual bravado and female degradation carried by the words don't do much for the Commonwealth of Puerto Rico's image, let alone forward the ad's argument that drinkers should switch to rum.

Advertisers, whether or not they consciously intend to, often use sexual-status displays of dominance to sell their products. In-

terestingly, the submissive female-rump presentation is used to signal subordination by both genders to superiors of both genders, so when Driver brand jeans uses a mammalian-rump display as the central image of its ad, it's difficult to separate all the players whose needs for dominant status are being expressed. For instance, at the very least, the advertiser places itself in the male superior position, although it is possible that some women in the target market might identify with the dominant role in Driver's imagery.

In the world of primitive cultures, New Guinea tribesmen attach foot-long tubes to their penises. In the world of civilized advertisers, Pierre Cardin man's cologne, shaped unmistakably like a phallus, is shown in an ad as a dominance display object of a superior male who is admired by his subordinates: "You wear it well."

In this case, hyperphallic packaging combines with power-message advertising. The guy is visibly a big player. (Comfortable in a tux.) Hardworking, smart, suave. (Reading his speech? Briefing himself for a diplomatic reception? Prepping for tomorrow's contest with Manly Power in a Man's World?) He has nouveaux tastes. (Checker-patterned linoleum —*very* classy.) Could be married or single. (The ring finger is neatly concealed.) Nothing particularly effeminate, but no women to be seen either.

And that's important, because this phallic-shaped bottle of men's perfume should hit two markets, straight and gay, if all goes well.

The phallic symbol, for anyone for whom it resonates, stands up and says precisely what it is without any embarrassment about what it's doing. If the straight male prefers to ignore the blatant hard-on in the foreground, the ad gives him permission to do so. If the gay male responds to the obvious suggestiveness, that's okay too. It's a clever male-manipulation ad, not least of all because it allows both markets to get their own messages without catering to either specifically.

Guess Jeans is one of those advertisers with a huge stake in the attraction of some women to the sadomasochistic side of sexuality, and the women it's after are young. Until quite recently, the campaign featured highly provocative black-and-white photos of porcelain-skinned girls in a string of seemingly endless encounters with salacious older men, labeled only by the scribbled red-lipsticked script "Georges Marciano" or "Guess Jeans."

Some of the more notorious scenes in Guess ads along the way include an aging Mafioso-type wearing sunglasses, in postures of sexual dominance toward young, semibuttoned women with apathetic expressions. One has us facing the kneeling rear of a woman looking up at the crotch of a man standing above her, arms folded expectantly. Although she *is* wearing a Guess jeans jacket, what is actually being advertised here? In most of the Guess ads, the advertiser's product is simply a prop for the center-stage interplay between the fragile, loosened-clothing, exposed vulnerability of a

nubile female and a possessive, unsavory Daddy-like male, as we see in one of the car scenes. Evocative of Louis Malle's 1978 film *Pretty Baby*, or Elia Kazan's earlier *Baby Doll* (1956), Guess is associating an edge of danger with its brand name, a strategy that plays directly on the urgency and ambivalence of adolescents' sexual impulses. Much of the time, the Guess girls look like runaways photographed in distasteful situations their mothers would never approve of.

Irresponsible? Guess jeans sell. The advertiser has gone to whatever lengths it takes to get noticed by its market and has been handsomely rewarded by the public. Some teenagers, like my daughter Julie's friend Alison, buy Guess jeans because "they're comfortable." But for others, the imagery does more than persuade them to wear the brand; the broader effects of

this kind of advertising fall outside of the narrow realm of marketing and into the larger universe of moral issues. The psychological messages sent by Guess imagery strongly imply that girls can use their sexuality to free themselves from parental constraints. The ads create the illusion that being possessed by a powerful, older man can be a glamorous identity for a confused, angry adolescent. Being used sexually, or running away, isn't portrayed as

being either self-destructive or hostile; it's presented as a daring walk on the rebel side of the tracks. The perfect counter to the ruling party of adults. The latest from Guess? Young women are still often portrayed as sexually submissive and dominated in ads, but now the man strong-arming her from behind while she straddles him and his motorcycle is as young as she.

In Revlon's internally produced ad for its Trouble fragrance, the psychological message isn't one of female submission, but rather one of equality between the sexes—both are equally ignorant. In plunging black décolletage, she smiles dreamily, conspiratorially, at her audience. The object of her designs leans on a bar in the shadows, wearing black, a fashionably decadent stubble, and slightly narrowed eyes. The headline titles this scene "He's Trouble, But He's Finally Met His

Match." What qualities does she bring to this sexual showdown? If she's sufficiently doused herself with Trouble, she's unhinged whatever mental apparatus might have stopped her from stepping into a story designed to come to a ruinous end. With Revlon's help, she'll match him in destructiveness. Trouble, the imagery tells consumers, can loosen the bothersome intellectual controls that so often interfere with romantic meetings at bars. As the copy explains, Trouble is "The fragrance for those times when your better judgment is better off ignored. After all, a little Trouble keeps life interesting."

How can all these images of sexual entanglings be going on in the eighties? Hasn't anyone told advertisers about AIDS? Over the years, I've frequently had the opportunity of being asked to comment on trends in advertising. The effect of the AIDS tragedy on the culture has been one of the year's hottest topics. Often, conclusions come to me masquerading as questions such as: What do you think about the new trend in advertising toward love and romance? What I think is that, given the sheer magnitude of print and broadcast messages, advertising "trends" are more often created by the media feeding off its own perceptions than reflecting a true groundswell of change in the industry.

While it is true that some advertisers have modified their explicitly young-and-sexual imagery to better reach maturing baby boomers engaged in long-term, committed romantic relationships, these instances can easily be counterbalanced by examples of advertisers calling for attention on the same old hormone hotline. There is little doubt that a combination of AIDS and aging has intensified the desire of people in our culture for lasting, substantive relationships, where two people fall in love and grow old together. Hollywood has jumped on this bandwagon and produced rashes of films, such as *Baby Boom, Three Men and a Baby, For Keeps*, and *She's Having a Baby*—that not only deemphasize the joys of promiscuity, but elevate to near-mythic wonder the pleasures of child rearing. These movies reflect a natural consequence of the inevitable winding down of the prolonged adolescence of the sixties. Again, while there are some noticeable recent changes in the culture's images of relationships, I believe that these do not eclipse the emphasis on sexuality that has been so pervasive in the media; instead, they provide some balance in a cultural marketing mix long skewed toward the sexual sell.

JOHNS+GORMAN FILMS IS NOW OPEN
FOR BUSINESS IN NEW YORK CITY.

We love L.A. But New York is where the action is.
So call Michael Calderin, the man in charge of our East Coast operation.
He'll do almost anything for those great, simple concepts. Almost.
JOHNS+GORMAN FILMS
305 Second Avenue, Penthouse, New York, NY 10003 · 212/677-4600

Not that the sexual sell is all bad. Sometimes it's entirely appropriate for the product, like sexy underwear, but even in a time when irresponsible sex is being linked with death, images of sin and suggestion continue to be a source of merriment for all kinds of advertisers. Johns + Gorman Films isn't too proud to play. The film-production company people solicit business from advertising agencies the old-fashioned way—they pimp for it. Their promotional ad is tongue-in-cheek, but it's difficult to put much stock in the possibility of real change in advertisers' sexual imagery when one of their image-makers introduces itself by placing the announcement "Johns + Gorman Films Is Now Open for Business in New York City" under a black-and-white photo of a proto-typical pair of prostitutes, ripped stockings and all, standing on a littered street corner looking for work!

One psychological development cropping up increasingly in ad imagery has little to do with romance in the traditional, interpersonal sense of the word. Some people find it safer to relate simply to themselves—and the monstrosity of AIDS looms as a conveniently unassailable reason to stay isolated. The myth of Narcissus lives.

Handsome Narcissus was extraordinarily enamored of his beauty. Although young maidens loved him, he paid no attention to any of them. Echo, a lovely nymph, was so pained by his coldness that she faded away, leaving only her voice, hopelessly repeating the last syllables of words it heard. The gods, angry at Narcissus because Echo was their favorite, punished him by making him fall in love with his own reflection in a pool. Despairing because he could never possess what he loved, he killed himself with a knife. The narcissus flower grew from the drops of his blood.

Calvin Klein's ad for Calvin Klein fragrance for men is a perfect contemporary rendition of the classical myth of Narcissus. Shot in black-and-white, sleekly oblong, the product has the form of a brick bullion—the same kind of gold that gilds the frame of the mirror in the photo—a mirror into which the transfixed, mes-merized face of a man enraptured by his own image is staring. He

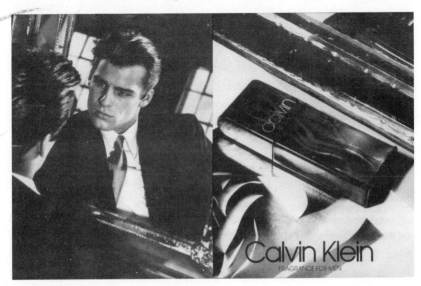

looks as if he could stay there forever. Clearly, this is the face of a man in love—and he only has eyes for himself. Homoerotic undertones aside, this is what narcissistic self-absorption is all about. Psychologically, it's a dead-end street.

At the root of this kind of narcissism are feelings of worthlessness, the inability to live up to unattainable expectations coupled with an insatiable need to extract admiration from others. Legions of advertisers use imagery that is ostensibly designed to be sexually provocative but that actually sets up a self-perpetuating cycle of narcissistic needs.

People in desperate need of validation from others are caught in a media avalanche of narcissistic images of people who essentially feel empty and unlovable beneath their grandiose postures. The sole purpose of these images is to persuade people that the way to achieve the sexual and personal power reflected by a commercial model is to buy the associated product. Consumers buy the product unconsciously hoping that they will win the admiration they covet, but since they're still trying to measure up to somebody else's expectations, they feel just as empty as ever on the inside. The process continues to fuel the quest for approval, which, in turn, fuels the sales of products selling a promise of narcissistic gratification.

Cecilia is newly divorced, thirty-five, and childless. She was married to an extremely wealthy, extremely self-involved real estate developer, and she never really expected much more than money and a spectacular escort out of the relationship. Finally, Cecilia acquired enough self-esteem to take a stand against her husband's frequenting various mistresses. At that point, Jordan divorced her. Cecilia married Jordan without the slightest idea about how to have a close relationship, but convincingly played the cultured and amusing wife at the endless rounds of social functions they attended.

To hear Cecilia tell it, it sounds as though she and Jordan spent a great deal of time talking about parties they were about to attend, or about to give, while primping in front of separate dressing-room mirrors. Although she feels there was no real problem with their sex life during her marriage, Cecilia admits that she felt detached and sometimes couldn't tell whether or not she'd had an orgasm with Jordan. Now, Cecilia has no interest in even dating, let alone in getting married again. On the surface, she claims she's terrified of getting AIDS. Underneath, she's terrified of getting any more intimate with a man than she did with Jordan. Her narcissism is her bodyguard.

Harper's Bazaar uses narcissistic self-absorption to interest female consumers in buying the magazine. The campaign, using no copy at all, focuses on pictures of women so locked into reading a copy of *Bazaar* that they are completely oblivious to the activities of the man, however unusual, in the same room. In one, a nude man is shown in the shower, vainly kissing the glass door—talk about protection!—to get the attention of a young woman in pearls and cocktail dress, engrossed in reading the magazine. The campaign, created by Margeotes-Fertitta & Weiss, Inc., is intended to be provocative, startling, slick, alienated, and ironic. But what is most arresting to me about the imagery is the level of narcissism and distance displayed by the women. The men might as well be pieces of furniture for all the interest they stir. And from Cecilia's perspective, and that of others like her, that's the safest way to play it.

A similarly aloof dynamic between men and women is used to sell a very different product—Procter & Gamble's Secret Dry Roll-On deodorant. In a campaign, created by Leo Burnett U.S.A. to communicate the brand's long-standing position: "Strong enough for a man but pH-balanced for a woman," a series of fashionably dressed female models, shot in color, are juxtaposed on larger-than-life black-and-white photos of muscular, sweaty male bodies. In one of these ads, the ultrafeminine, pink-

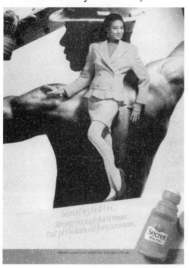

suited, white-stockinged woman beams with self-satisfaction as she appears to lean against the dripping, rippling, massive back of a hard-hatted construction worker. Fearlessly, she looks out at her audience, secure in the certainty that no matter how big or how wet or how strong this man is, she'll remain utterly untouched—utterly composed. Pink-gloved hands outstretched as if drying her nails, one knee bent demurely, the ultimate lady is thoroughly protected from being sullied by the slightest contact with primal man.

Secret's marketing message: Regardless of the intensity of a woman's perspiration, the product will keep her dry. The psychological message: It is best to stay in control, to turn away from strong sexual feelings, and to be emotionally uninvolved. Notably, both of these messages are congruent with the highly repressive attitudes toward smell in our society. Smell is strongly associated with sexuality in the majority of mammals, and research into one of the chemical components of perspiration (pheromones) points to scent acting as a primary sexual attractor. Napoleon is on record as having written to his wife Josephine, "I'm coming home—don't wash for three days." A culture that has produced a mammoth industry founded entirely on the control of rampant human body odor and its concomitant ardor is, hypothetically, heavily invested in curbing primitive urges. The deodorant industry gains its strength from unconscious fears. Using images that, perhaps, inadvertently exploit an emerging need for even greater distance from the threat of sexuality, Secret indirectly pro-

motes psychological repression.

Even perfume advertising, which, given the nature of the product's intrinsic sensuality, has appropriately featured traditional imagery suggestive of romantic or sexually charged interludes, abounds with examples of pure self-indulgence and smug egocentricity rather than relationships. Elizabeth Arden is the sublicenser of Fendi perfume, and its advertising is dominated by a

luminous photograph of a beautiful woman, eyes closed in the passion of the moment, kissing the marble lips of a sculptured male bust. No risk of messy intimate exposure with this packaged smell. The message is resoundingly clear on the subject of emotional closeness: Don't do it. Stick with statues and cozy up to a healthy hunk of alabaster and you won't get hurt. Here, any sexuality resides exclusively on Fantasy Island, an island inhabited by the very embodiment of a nonthreatening male with no needs of his own: a Roman statue.

At least in Secret's ad, there is a certain amount of sexual tension in the imagery, the suggestion of human relationship; after all, if she did lose her cool, she'd run smack up against raw, living, male hormones. With Fendi, she could go ape wild with, as the copy calls it, *"la passione di Roma,"* and the object of her desires would remain as stone cold as the day he was carved. Fendi romanticizes emotional distance and sells a lot of perfume on the basis of an image that elevates lack of commitment and the psychological avoidance of real intimacy to an art form.

Although Calvin Klein Cosmetic Corporation's use of sexual imagery in advertising, from the earlier Obsession through the more recent Eternity brands of fragrances, appears, on the surface, to have moved from uncommitted, self-centered couplings toward visions of mature, mutual relationships, underneath the seemingly disparate images runs a common thread that sends a consistent message to the public. Despite Calvin Klein's assiduous efforts to package the personalities of Obsession and Eternity differently, the advertiser's family album of brands is still filled with people who appear incapable of having a relationship with a person separate from themselves.

Consider Calvin Klein's Obsession perfume. When it's ménage-à-many ads first broke, the intentionally scandalous, enormously successful campaign was met with a combination of titillation and outrage, depending on how well the imagery fit into the sexual fantasies of the viewer. Grainy, chiaroscuro nudes of all genders, sensuously coupled in all configurations, formed the backdrop for the print ads; commercials ended with a man's voice achingly murmuring, "Ah! The smell of it!" The use of the word "smell," with its primitive biological connotations, rather than the more usual "scent" or "fragrance," cued even more basic sexuality for Obsession, creating a brand personality built on the free expression of basic human lust.

Obsession's smell is strongly musky, a scent categorized by perfumers as "animalic" because of its organic source, and is quite recognizable on the wearer. I am regularly struck by the range of women I pass during a day whose choice of perfume message to send is Obsession's. Many are far from young, and far from the media-based definition of sexy, but they're doused with a scent-image that reveals their underlying fantasies of themselves—fantasies nourished by advertising.

Not long ago, I was in a Saks Fifth Avenue and an unmistakable current of Obsession wafted by, trailed by an energetic, pink-haired, cosmetic-laden matron with hat and gloves. While it is true that, demographically, women of her age tend to wear heavier fragrances, that's not the whole show. Perfume advertising is all image —that's what drives the product category. At some level, here was a woman with a fantasy of herself as a femme fatale—a lasciv-

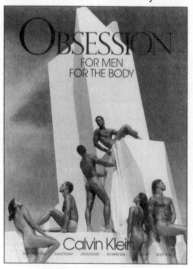

ious consort—in secret longing.

After the mating-hydra approach to selling Obsession, a shift occurs in the brand's advertising imagery. What do we have next? A bunch of naked people who studiously avoid contact of any kind with each other. In one ad for Obsession, four muscular men and two well-toned women organize their oiled, nude bodies into approximate pairs—not all of which include one member of the opposite sex—on and about a tall, aggressively angled white obelisk. Any sign of emotion, let alone sexual passion, has been eradicated. The people are turned stiffly away from each other, posturing states of grand boredom—noses hoisted in the air as if listening to a private muse. These people have no more feelings or thoughts going on than the phallic prop they surround. What's being sold here is an elaborate image of self-control through psychological detachment. It's as if only two poles of the erotic continuum can be conceptualized by Obsession's advertiser—unbounded promiscuity or asexual androidism. The real obsession is again with the self, which is certainly one way of pulling back from messy, possibly even disease-carrying, relationships, with no expectations of closeness that counts. That's a fairly discouraging cultural mirror.

Calvin Klein's Eternity, the advertiser's latest fragrance entry, uses advertising that creates the impression that the image of this product is radically different from the type of flagrant sexual displays associated with Obsession—and they are, but only on the surface. In one of the introductory print ads, a married couple,

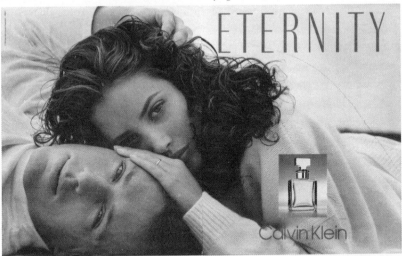

ring glinting in evidence, rest against one another, beneath the word "Eternity," written in classic typeface; in others, the couple are joined by their children in tranquil settings. Squeakily wholesome commitment and tender romance look like the new name of the game, until the characters play out a bizarre view of what their relationship might really be about in Eternity's *television* campaign.

In Eternity's series of surrealistic, technically superb spots, a man and woman voice their fears of being engulfed and consumed by the fervor of their cravings for each other. Speaking in the hollow, hurried flatness of an Ingmar Bergman film, the lovers engage in ardent psychological jargon about the frightening nature of their hopelessly enmeshed relationship. They say things like "We haven't hurt each other yet, but we soon will. . . ."; "Help me destroy me—become me until there's nothing left but you. . . ."; "I destroy everything I love. . . ."; "I don't know where I end and you begin . . . would you still love me if I were a woman?"; and the familiar narcissistic refrain, "When I look at you, I feel like I'm looking in a mirror."

This isn't love, and it isn't romance; this is an *obsession*, an addiction. With this type of psychological message, the advertiser's imagery may be moving away from multiple naked sex partners, but the model of narcissistic self-involvement is just as entrenched as ever. The romantic potential of these ads is mired in the fears of the emotional risks of closeness, fears that are often rooted in a poorly defined self-identity. For the commercials' heroes, spending an eternity together—Eternity's promise—would be tantamount to a hereafter in Sartre's *No Exit*.

Advertisers aren't the cause of people's problems with true intimacy, but neither are they the passive, neutral reflectors of how our society views relationships. In their frenzied bids for attention, advertisers frequently wave sexual imagery at consumers, hoping to be remembered. Some are; many are not. But what does get set in the collective memory of the culture are portraits of stunted sexual development, portraits of sexual-status displays, narcissistic glorification, and crude innuendo, portraits that are sold along with products pledging to help consumers put themselves in the power positions promoted by the advertiser as enviable.

Because these portraits reflect essentially insecure identities, the images promoted point the way toward more, rather than less, emotional emptiness. When Madison Avenue's idea of a loving relationship includes mutual self-destruction, the measuring-up game can become downright crippling. Ideally, relationships are strongest when both partners play with a full deck, with a sense of security and solid identity. Barring that, it's a safer bet to play with fewer cards than to borrow advertisers' pictures and try to build a winning hand from them.

CHAPTER 8

CASHING IN ON KIDS

About the second month of a baby's life, when seemingly end-less feedings, diaperings, and pacings have cranked the new parents' frazzle level to an electric high and driven them to fleetingly con-sider trading her in at the local pet shop, the baby smiles. It isn't just one of those random smiles that occasionally tag along with a sneeze or burp—she smiles *back* at her parents.

Ingenuous design. There's a powerful psychological function in that wonderful, irresistible smile. It's nature's lock on survival. And it works because it's part of our psychobiological makeup to be suckers for kids.

So it's no accident that children in advertising are notoriously superb attention-grabbers. That's one of their biggest job assign-ments in life, and it's our job to respond.

It's no secret that children, particularly at their Saturday morn-ing wide-eyed best, are primed for parent-pleading by cartoon shows that are little more than program-length commercials for toy characters and by blizzards of spots entertaining enough to young minds to be virtually indistinguishable from the shows nes-tled around them. But what happens when advertisers use kids, *not* to pitch products to *them,* but to persuade an *adult* market to buy *adult* products?

Sticking a picture of an adorable child into an ad practically guarantees that a wide variety of humans will at least look at it. But beyond that, cashing in on kids' smiles as a way of getting adults to open their wallets along with their hearts, isn't as sure a bet for advertisers as it might look. The playground is full of pitfalls for advertisers, who often attempt to engage the public with all the subtlety of a stranger enticing a well-warned youngster with a bag of gumdrops; and pitfalls for viewers, who may be troubled about how an ad uses kids, and end up feeling vaguely uncomfortable when they find themselves not liking a perfectly adorable child; and pitfalls for kids, who are often pushed toward adulthood by parents who may not have bought the product, but have unwittingly bought an image of children as short grown-ups.

Simply because kids do have the power to evoke profound emotions in us, advertisers need to be very clear about exactly what they're saying about their product, whom they're saying it to, and what image they're using to send their message. Often advertisers aren't clear, either in terms of cultural or market effects; ads misfire and advertisers wonder why, when riveting attention with a delightful little face seems to hold out such certain success.

Traditionally, agencies incorporate images of children in ads in the hope of profiting from consumers' natural fondness for kids. Advertisers "borrow" interest in children to move products. When used with warmth, sensitivity, and an understanding of the psychological dynamics involved, kids can make us feel favorably disposed toward a whole gamut of products that the advertiser wants us to love. But overlooking subtle details can sour the sell.

A few years ago, Wells, Rich, Greene created a Pan American World Airways campaign, which uses the magnetism of babies in a confusing way. Beaming forth from the competitive clutter of other airlines' rational statements about rates and benefits, the emotional power of Pan Am's cheerful cherub is lost on the business reader—its purported audience. The advertiser attempts to anchor the interest it borrows from the baby by conceptualizing the money spent on its new service as a new birth: "Pan Am Proudly Announces the Arrival of Our Million Dollar Baby." There's no getting around the essential lovableness of the baby in the picture. But plopping a pilot's hat on her darling little head doesn't automatically bestow relevance on her role in aviation.

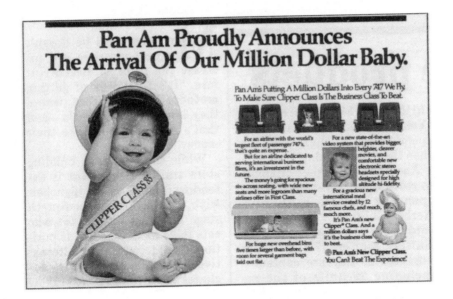

Pan Am's "Million Dollar Baby" is designed to make its Clipper Class "The Business Class to Beat." So the ad is targeted specifically to business travelers, people who may well have kids, but who aren't supposed to be thinking family vacation when they— Pan Am hopes—read the copy describing such benefits as "electronic stereo headsets" and "12 famous chefs." At this point, the baby's anchor to the product starts to drift, regardless of how many smiles her salute elicits. Then things get a bit more complicated.

In the Pan Am piece, the agency wanted the photogenic baby's diminutive size to highlight the 747's spaciousness, a strategy that works beautifully when the wee one is waving happily from an airplane seat.

But the use of this same baby triggers disquieting associations when she appears *inside* the overhead bin. Parents of small children, whether or not they are the *intended* targets, do make up a significant part of the business market. This market—consciously or not—has been sensitized to the dangers of suffocation posed by an enclosure such as a freezer, which bears a too-close-for-comfort similarity to the overhead bin. Not to mention the fear of falling. And certainly not to mention how much the bin resembles a coffin. The point is, an airplane luggage bin is not a safe place for a baby to play.

Della Femina, Travisano & Partners' print piece for First Boston Bank, which symbolizes the advertiser as "The $40 Billion

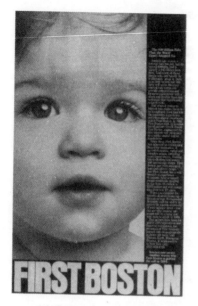

FIRST BOSTON

Baby That the World Hasn't Adopted Yet," is also a few years old, but right in step with the current industry rage—babies in ads. Almost everyone involved—agency and advertiser alike—can feel good inside about such a heartwarming image of interest-rate swaps. And who but the most unrepentant Scrooge among consumers could, as those doe-eyed, feed-the-hungry photos dare, just turn the page without a responsive heart-tug? The ad fairly throbs with humanism. So far, so good.

But sometimes interest borrowed from as engaging an infant as First Boston's can dip the creditor into the red. The proportionally huge face dominating the ad carries such emotional high voltage that it threatens to overwhelm the rational copy points carried in the tiny, dense print. Good-bye, intellectual circuits. People's mental fuses blow when they're immersed in a wonderful—or awful—feeling, and their number-crunching capacity to process a heavy surge of digital-banking data shuts down.

Despite these problems, borrowing interest from babies is hot news that's getting even hotter in the advertising industry. Both the Ford and Wilhelmina modeling agencies recently opened pre-toddler divisions in New York, and have been deluged with casting calls for their new crops. Until media and marketing mavens decided that a *bona fide* trend was afoot (meaning that last hurrah, baby-bearing in thirtyish couples, was noticed and hyped sufficiently to alleviate marketers' malaise over having no new consumer hot buttons to push) two-year-olds were about as young as modeling agencies accepted. But when advertisers start asking for babies, babies they get.

Michelin is generally credited with precipitating the proliferation of babies in ads with its 1985 launch of a still-running, highly successful tire campaign, developed at DDB Needham. Instead of the usual tire-tread-and-car-performance shots, the commercials show only a baby (or babies, as more and more vignettes have been developed) crawling or sitting or playing in and around a Michelin tire. Behind these visuals, the only sounds are of a conversation between two adults, in which one questions the wisdom of spending extra money on tires ("a tire's a tire") while the other cites Michelin's merits ("my last set of Michelins got sixty thousand miles"). The spots conclude with an announcer's voice behind a final shot of baby-in-tire, pointing out the only reason for purchase that really matters: "Michelin. Because so much is riding on your tires."

Gripping, yet very gentle. Penny-pinching parents watching the Michelin spots would be hard-pressed to use the economics excuse not to buy the product after such a powerful emotional equivalence of love and tire reliability. The campaign has sold mountains of Michelins, and has

done so primarily by appealing not to the thrill-a-minute, eat-the-road mind-set many of its competitors promote, but by focusing on a completely different psychological bottom line in its market.

Jack Mariucci, DDB Needham's executive creative director and the art director on the Michelin campaign, is proud of the concept he originated. Realizing my question was a little like asking a centipede which leg it moves first, I asked him about the creative process behind his breakthrough idea. Mr. Mariucci recalled wanting to show something quite different from the usual road's-point-of-view tire ads. And then he came up with the image of a gentle child together with a hard rubber tire. The baby, Mr. Mariucci commented, is "the purest part of yourself—you *are* that child and all of *that* is riding on your tires."

I have tremendous respect and admiration for the creative leap. Beyond my fascination with the psychological interplay between us and advertising, I love the astounding creativity in great ads. Great because they're so funny or shocking or moving or artistic or, as in the case of Michelin, so human. There was no question about how the children were to be used in the spots and it's this commitment to portraying them without artifice—with their basic humanity—that sets the campaign so far apart from so many other advertisers' kiddie shows. In the Michelin Campaign, babies are supposed to be babies. They aren't supposed to be posed or prodded or propped.

Psychologically and ethically, the campaign is on a plane of maturity that has broader cultural values than its considerable leverage as a sales tool. And it has captured every major advertising award.

Babies are universal carriers of strong emotional ties for humans—they're natural. And as long as they are allowed to retain their naturalness, just by being themselves, they retain their most fundamental power to connect. With one exception, Michelin's little ones go about being adorable by just being babies.

The one exception to Michelin's let-babies-be-babies approach to its campaign is "Hot Wheels," a spot designed for the sports-car market. In this one, a baby girl, accompanied by a boy in sunglasses, "drive" a tire around, but this time *they're* doing the talking. And what they're talking about sounds like a conversation between teenagers reveling in the thrills of fast driving. Not only does the girl admire the boy's macho-performance automobile ("What did you do to your car, Joey? It's really *hot*")—a position that inadvertently reinforces the cultural fantasy that speed is sexy—she ends up being chased by a baby cop as well.

Undoubtedly, the advertiser intended only for this strategy to reach the sports-car market in a cute way, consistent with the rest of the Michelin campaign. It may be cute, but it casts babies in roles that mimic a certain recklessness of driving behavior.

If "so much is riding on your tires," why promote Michelin within the context of *babies* being flagged down by the police? The spot may resonate with sports-car drivers' enthusiasm for the fast lane, but it aligns itself with its market by using imagery that attaches a playful cops-and-robbers quality to "hot" driving. But there was no deliberate intent to promote speeding through the spot's imagery. The anomaly of "Hot Wheels" aside, few advertisers use babies with as much sensitivity and product relevance as Michelin, but even Michelin can sometimes produce advertising that sends an unintentionally confusing message about kids.

Renée is a thirty-year-old accountant with a busy center-city firm. Like so many professional women in our society, she's in the midst of a critical life decision—whether to have a baby now and necessarily jump the track on her career, wait until she's more firmly established and *then* start a family, or forget the whole idea and chug straight ahead to the promised land of ever-increasing success. She knows she's a first-rate accountant and has the promotions to prove it, but being a mother is a complete unknown. The pushes and pulls in Renée's life are complex and often contradictory, as they are for so many women trying to make this decision in similar circumstances: a good marriage in which both partners give each other plenty of room, a thriving career, parents yearning to dote on grandchildren, affection for children (unless they're trampolining the seats near her on a business trip), fear of being a homebody like her mother, jealousy of her friends' pregnancies, and a relentlessly ticking biological clock. To Renée, this decision is the hardest and most serious that she has ever had to face in her adult life.

This is the decision Chevrolet chooses to compare with buying a car. In a print ad created by Lintas: Campbell-Ewald (which appeared in *Ms.* magazine, among others!), the top two thirds of a double-page spread consists of a dreamily out-of-focus photo of a mother looking off into the distance, holding an infant. In the black band across the bottom, the headline admonishes, "Don't

spend the next six years wondering if you did the right thing."
What does the advertiser suggest to women as a way of resolving
this ambivalence? The copy offers the solution: "In a world full
of doubt, it's nice to know there are still some things you can
count on. . . . Bring home a new Chevy, any new Chevy, and
you can count on a 6-year, 60,000-mile (whichever comes first)
warranty. . . ."

Forget about the baby, Renée, you'd be better off with a new
car. Besides, babies don't come with warranties; if you get a lemon,
you're stuck with it. And even if you get a good one, the "next
six years," according to Chevy, would probably *still* be filled with
lingering doubts. Doesn't all this make Chevy look better and
better?

Chevrolet's transparent attempt to bait women buyers by holding up a warm fuzzy fantasy of motherhood, voicing their deepest
doubts, and then switching to Chevy as the superior choice ridic-
ulously reduces the decision to have a baby as analogous to the
decision to buy a new set of wheels. Further stacking the deck, that
set of wheels—that Chevy—is photographed in the sharp-edged focus of reality, in contrast to the vaporous baby shot. Visually, the
message is that the car is real, attainable, solid; the baby is just a
dream. Solve life's untidy problems with consumer goods.

One of the ads in an ongoing campaign for Johnnie Walker,
using attractive, young, upscale, probably professional women to
pitch the liquor, blithely skips
down the same thorny path to
their hearts and pocketbooks as
Chevrolet does, except no child
is pictured. In the piece, created
by Smith Greenland, Inc., two
women are shown warmly chat-
ting beneath the line "He's crazy
about my kid. *And* he drinks
Johnnie Walker." Presumably,
she's been through a divorce, has
a child, and has met a man who
she believes actually likes her child.
Her good fortune brims all over
her face. But this woman, we are

asked to believe, attaches the same importance to the gentleman's fondness for her offspring as to his preference for Johnnie Walker. People don't talk like this, and people don't think like this.

Johnnie Walker's misguided efforts to entreat baby boomers to identify with imagery equating brand choice with emotional attachment for a child, and Chevrolet's breezy dismissal of the angst of decision-making with a wave of its warranty, exemplify advertisers trying hard to cash in on kids but coming up short—very short—in registering and understanding human emotions. They both seem to think that consumers will love the advertisers' babies—their carefully nurtured and pampered brands—at least as much as their own. Although it's insulting, this isn't particularly damaging to the public; it's more a case of advertisers shooting themselves in the foot while trying to make the consumer dance.

On the other hand, when advertisers use kids directly as shills, the psychological and cultural influences are more complex—and more negative—than when they're used as a shortcut to borrow interest for a product or as an ingratiating reflection of a particular target market's stage in life (hoping to get consumers to see themselves in the pretty picture that, naturally, includes the brand). When children are used as shills for adult products, they tend to be packaged as pint-sized adults, a strategy that can easily backfire in marketing and is nearly a sure bet for problems in the real world of parenting.

Kids in this culture are suffering from a loss of the time and permission just to be kids, and advertisers winding kids up to hawk their products are selling persuasive images that endorse and fuel the acceleration of childhood. The grow-up-quick ads aimed at adults use kids who are costumed to look older, more "adult" than they really are. Made-up little girls looking almost as sexy as Mommy crop up everywhere. They're meltingly cute—the modeling agencies see to that—but when they begin putting on blush, eyeliner, shadow, and lipstick, the effects can get bizarre.

Kaiser-Roth Hosiery's commercial for Ultra Sense mixed adult and child psychological messages in a way that was supposed to capture the woman's hosiery market. According to Betty Freedman, creative director/copywriter at the time at Grey Advertising, New York, the concept of a little girl selling "luxury" evolved out of "digging back into childhood experiences" and recalling the

"wonder" of watching mother's dressing rituals.

The intent was to create a nontraditional piece of advertising that would show luxury and femininity through a child's eyes. In short, the spot was designed to conjure up delightful childhood memories for its target audience.

In choosing to employ a child as a shill in advertising, certain artifices, such as referring to brand names as if they were part of everyday speech, betray the adult machinery behind the process. In the spot, the little girl holds up the product and says in her tiny voice, "These are her [Mommy's] panty hose—Ultra Sense—they feel *smooth*," as she caresses a pair of women's legs sidling up to her hand.

In this case, the little girl isn't just selling "luxurious" panty hose, she's also selling adult sensuality—illustrated by her mother's seductive posings throughout the spot. The daughter, who implicitly invites the *adult* audience to "watch Mommy dressing" along with her, throws a curve ball into the campaign's playing field.

In trying to simultaneously convey both adult *and* child sensuality, a potentially disturbing, albeit subconscious, situation is suggested. This is a spot in which a little girl observes, "My mommy has beautiful legs—Daddy says so," while "Mommy" languidly stretches up her leg on the bed. After all, *Daddy* is supposed to be caressing and talking up Mommy's silky, smooth legs.

Maybelline came up with another kind of cozy mother-daughter ad. In an ad for Brush/Blush, created by DDB Needham Worldwide in Chicago, the little girl is cheek by jowl with Mom. The kid is not overly made up, she wears a little girl's dress, and she's making no special attempt to lure the audience. The point of the ad has nothing to do with sexuality: The nonverbal closeness between the girl's complexion and the woman's complexion, together with the copy, say that both of them "blush beautifully, glow

naturally." The "moment in time," as the copy describes the scene, looks warm and is. The scrap of paper near the product reinforces "INNOCENT."

Why would women be drawn to Maybelline Brush/Blush after gazing at this ad? Although this lacks the pseudo-sexuality of the Ultra Sense ad, something analogous is subtly implied by the precious closeness between mother and daughter. The age gap is not so great after all, these ads suggest. Daughter can admire mother's panty hose; mother can have daughter's blushing and glowing complexion. It's all very buddy-buddy.

A clue to what's going on here might be in some current demographics; women are having children later, and there are more single mothers than ever before. I'm reminded of a client, Margaret, a divorced professional woman in her late thirties, who has a very strong, close relationship with her daughter, Eileen. The first time Margaret spoke about Eileen, she was effusive in praising the girl's "maturity." Margaret told me that Eileen was someone she could confide in. There were few secrets between them.

"I went through some very hard times after Bill [her husband] left me," Margaret said. "I haven't had an easy time with men since then. It's been on-again off-again, and sometimes I swear I'll never have another date in my life. I don't know what I'd do without Eileen. She tells me, 'Oh, Mom, it'll be okay.' She's great. She's really supportive in a lot of ways."

"How old is Eileen?" I asked.

"She's nine," said Eileen's mother.

Margaret is not atypical. I'd heard it before. And it makes sense: Kids in single-parent families do grow up fast. They have to take on more at an earlier age. If there's no spouse around and the parent and child are close, the child may get a large dose of adult confidences. A mother in these situations may not only treat her daughter like a little adult, she likes to *see* her daughter as a little adult—as a good companion and a real friend, as well as a child.

So these ads have appeal. The daughters are huggable, but they're also composed and mature. They're hanging out with Mom. They can relate to her concerns about panty hose, makeup . . . even perfume.

Where Maybelline uses some restraint with the kid, some advertisers break the sound barrier in propelling a child toward adulthood.

About five years ago, *Harper's Bazaar* ran a classic example of unintended sexualization, ostensibly in order to engender early interest in products. The magazine ran a photo feature on fragrances entitled "Tiny Treasures," the introduction to which read, "A woman's all-important scent memory begins to develop in earliest childhood." Photographed by Francesco Scavullo, who also created drop-dead seductress covers for *Cosmopolitan*, a beautiful little girl, naked from the waist up, her hair and face elegantly done up, was shown holding different brands of perfume.

Abandon all girlhood, ye who enter here. The Scavullo girl is not relating to a mommy at all. Instead, she's gazing directly at the reader with the wide-eyed gaze that we know so well from professionally seductive models. She is cast literally as a little adult, precisely mimicking the cosmetic style of a mature woman in our society. The child is gone.

Is this ad attractive to women? Will female consumers be offended by the deliberate sexualization of preteen models—or does the young facsimile establish a marketable bond with the much-older target reader?

A bond is there all right. Revlon has staked a campaign on it. In fact, a Revlon ad poses the ultimate farewell to notions of innocent girlhood.

Its series of ads for New Complexion Makeup uses close-up shots of four flawlessly beautiful international models as paragons of product benefits. In a recent piece, twelve-year-old Tara D'Am-

The most unforgettable women in the world wear REVLON

brosio, looking even younger, poses in the lineup of lavishly coiffed and made-up adult women photographed above the headline "The most unforgettable women in the world wear REVLON."

Why would an advertiser tell consumers that it is categorizing a lovely, preadolescent girl as an "unforgettable woman"? It seems to be, at the least, a blurring of the boundaries between children and adults, a blurring that represents a moral gray area to the culture. It is ethically and psychologically reprehensible to create the illusion that it's somehow permissible to treat little girls as if they were women. Beyond this, the copy positions Revlon's New Complexion Makeup: "At last, perfection." The ad's imagery beckons to parents striving to be perfect, not only through their own achievements, but through the perfection of their children. Be as indeterminate in age and "flawlessly perfect" as your child, who is a reflection of you; as the copy concludes, "Finally, you can have the complexion you wish you'd been born with."

All the marketing messages in the Revlon ad fit together—the symbolic child-as-adult/adult-as-child, the product as the way to achieve the mirage of perfection, and the needs of the female consumer—regardless of age—to measure up to the images of beauty promoted and designed by advertisers such as Revlon. But psychologically, the picture falls apart. It is clear from the photograph that Tara isn't just playing dress-up. Young girls treated as adult dolls end up being highly adept at being charming and enchanting, while inside they feel empty and estranged from their peers. Tara's a working girl; she's pictured in the midst of a very special peer group. Theoretically, she ought to be out riding her bike. But the viewer of this ad, which appears in women's magazines, whether mature or a struggling teen, gets the idea that we females are all in this together. Four gorgeous faces in the Revlon ad implore females in the society to enter their world—to become exquisite mannequins—to buy the fantasy and buy the makeup. Psychologically, the measuring-up process casts a broad net with this one; kids and adults hear Madison Avenue's siren song. Being alluring is what it's all about—at any age and at any price.

Kiddie ads can also stir pity, and something more, when they're aimed at the soft underbellies of doting parents.

AT 1 A.M., YOU'D BETTER HAVE A
NASAL DECONGESTANT THAT'S VERY FAST,
AND VERY EFFECTIVE.

An ad for Winthrop Laboratory's Neo-Synephrine uses a child to persuade parents to buy its cold medication, but in such a way that the pure and simple reality of kid-with-cold is used as a bridge to the diversity of feelings parents experience when faced with the presence of such a late-night visitor. Above the picture of a child, complete with stuffy nose, blanket, and Teddy, standing miserably in his parent's doorway is the challenge: "At 1 A.M. You'd Better Have a Nasal Decongestant That's Very Fast. And Very Effective." It's enough to make parents reevaluate, uneasily, their medical preparedness.

This ad's effectiveness lies in its psychological integrity. It engages its target because it reflects the range of parental emotions —from selfless, concerned caring all the way to selfish, exhausted desperation—that a sick child can arouse. The copy empathizes with both sides: "He's miserable and so are you."

Even without the copy, written by Cunningham & Walsh, New York, the ad's messages radiate from the child's doleful, trusting eyes and limp posture, as well as from the glowing backlighting, which makes him look like he's just landed there in the doorway on a special mission, which he has. That mission: Give me Neo-Synephrine quick or shove over, folks, I'm here for the night. A funny, true, and persuasive portrayal of a child used to sell a product.

But what happens when the product benefit is mental health, and the problem is far more serious than a case of the sniffles? Again, advertisers are more prepared than ever to pull heartstrings. With one advertiser, the emotional game is played with no holds barred. A life-and-death issue is slammed full force into the public's face.

The ad in question was sponsored by the Psychiatric Institute of Washington, and uses an emotional sledgehammer as its graphic message: a "suicide note" left by a child to his parents.

The letter format is a zinger because it exemplifies how kids, particularly kids who have trouble openly expressing their feelings, might try to "talk" to their parents. But in this case, the letter represents a message that came too late. The *content* of the "suicide note," which includes the guilt and apology and gratitude for "putting up with me" that is typical in suicidally depressed children, is right on the money. Clearly, the agency did its homework in that regard.

It is extremely difficult for parents—the targeted consumers in the Psychiatric Institute of Washington's ad—to entertain the thought

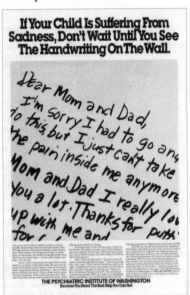

that their child's "sadness" could reflect a suicidal depression. The headline in the ad minces no words, makes no excuses, and issues a call for action *before* it's too late: "If Your Child Is Suffering from Sadness, Don't Wait Until You See the Handwriting on the Wall." Backing up the verbal warning is a graphic representation of exactly what "Handwriting on the Wall" means.

Getting people to pay attention to the existence of emotional problems in someone close to them is one of the most difficult jobs in psychotherapy. Breaking through the denial—through the veritable stone wall of defenses —might even be a tougher job for an advertiser, given the limited nature of the communication. Yet this is the challenge facing today's psychiatric institutions charged with making their staunchly defended target market aware of services that these potential customers do not believe they need or want.

Trying to penetrate the resistance and denial of loving but frightened relatives and friends by confronting them with reality involves risk. Confrontation may open a reservoir of defensive anger or withdrawal and lead to yet another breakdown in communications. And there's more. There's the underlying dynamics of a family unconsciously trying *not to see* the emotional problems of one of its members, because it may *need* the troubled individual to stay just the way he is in order to maintain the equilibrium of the unit. For example, by focusing all their attention on the diet of an obese child, parents can avoid looking at problems in their marriage. In such cases, exploring the emotional stress *behind* a problem such as childhood obesity carries the danger that effective therapy may disrupt the homeostasis of the family itself. In short, powerful psychological forces work against any efforts, either through advertising or interpersonal communications, to break down these resistances to facing hard truths about friends, relatives, or even oneself.

When dealing with massive denial, social mores of being "nice," "cautious," "tactful" or nonintrusive, simply don't work. The battle calls for brutal honesty, directness, and confrontation. And since mental illness can mean a matter of life and death, the tactics include whatever it takes to get through.

What it takes to get through needs to be psychologically arresting. The Psychiatric Institute of Washington has a highly charged product to sell—psychiatric services—and it's going for the parental jugular, raising questions we all fear to ask. Do we *really* know our children? Do we *really* pay attention to what they are thinking and feeling? Are we overlooking signs that they are drifting away from us (or reality) into realms of "sadness" or worse?

This ad is 180 degrees from the Revlon/Maybelline/Ultra Sense concept of the child as a knowledgeable, competent miniature adult. The "suicide note" (actually lettered by a commercial artist) warns us of the children who *can't* cope with an adult world, or any world. Whether or not the consumers (parents) hold any faith in the product in question (psychiatry), the ad makes its point by using an facsimile of a kid's note with shocking impact.

But using kids for shock value is a two-edged sword. If the shock effect goes too far, the audience gets polarized. Advertisers, of course, hope more of the audience is polarized *toward* the product than *away* from it, but the very thing that shocks may trigger jolts of adverse reactions.

In the Psychiatric Institute ad, for instance, the impact of the shock, at an unconscious level, is somewhat buffered by the in-authenticity of the handwritten message. A clinician would probably recognize that the handwriting is not really that of a child on the verge of suicide. But what about the effect of this artifice, in conjunction with the threatening tone of the message, on the lay public?

If some skeptic in the target audience begins to envision hordes of mothers with "sad" children being manipulated into signing up for $100-and-upward-an-hour therapy, *her* response to this shock-ing ad could deteriorate to a cynical—and maybe even dangerous —refusal to be swayed by its powerful message.

And the more questionable the product's value, the more po-tentially negative the impact of a shock strategy. In this department, one of my personal worst-taste-in-child-advertising awards goes

to DDB Needham, which created a Christmas toy ad for Eveready that features kid-as-terrorist to sell batteries. Dressing up a little boy in a hooded robe and dark glasses —carrying a blue machine gun (evidently one that requires bat-teries)—headlined, so there can be no mistaking the Middle East associations, "For a Blessed Christmas, You Need a Battery That Can Keep Up with a Holy Terror," isn't even slightly cute. No more than kids holding up banks with toy guns or getting

For A Blessed Christmas, You Need A Battery That Can Keep Up With A Holy Terror.

Super Heavy Duty

Eveready® Super Heavy Duty Batteries. All the power you need to get through the holidays. At a price that isn't heavy duty. Eveready Super Heavy Duty Batteries.

They Work. For You.

blown away by cops who mistake their plastic firearms for the real thing is cute.

Eveready reaches the bottom of the barrel in the way it uses a kid in advertising. But there are good kid ads around, if one looks long enough. One of my favorites is a commercial created by Lewis Gilman & Kynett, for Silo, a discount TV and appliance chain, for its Christmas campaign.

 Silo's "Five Kids" spot consists of quick cameos of each kid talking directly to the viewer about what he or she wants, as if answering the seasonal question put to children. They're nicely dressed up, as though they're visiting relatives for the holidays, and are well-mannered without being ingratiating. The spot isn't advertising specific products, and the kids aren't depicted as greedy little sophisticates coveting big-ticket electronic toys for adults.

In the Silo spot, a curly redheaded girl clasps her hands unselfconsciously and has high hopes for humanity: "I want everyone in the world to be happy." Making upside-down goggles on his eyes with his fingers, a boy says gleefully, "And I want X-ray eyes." "I *want* ballet lessons," a muscular little guy says, thumping his chest, "you got a problem with that?" Another pulls no punches in stating his—and so many other kids'—heart's desire: "I want to be an only child." In a serious, sincere voice, one little girl requests, "I want a color TV—with remote," in the only product reference in the commercial, which then cuts to a blue gift box marked with the advertiser's name. Then, the only adult voice in the spot makes the sales reference: "Silo—where you know you can get at least one thing on your list." But the spot doesn't close on that sales message, although it could have and still have maintained the integrity of the advertiser's use of kids. It closes with the curly redhead saying, "And, if possible, I'd like it to snow," while she wiggles her fingers down from the sky.

I wondered what kinds of reactions the campaign got from the public. Charles Jacoby, Silo's director of advertising, reports receiving several hundred calls and letters over the two seasons the spots aired. People love the warmth and uniqueness of the commercials and they have favorites among the kids, like the wiggly-fingered snow girl and the tough guy who wants ballet lessons.

How did the Silo campaign's creators get such naturalness from its young actors? Lines and actions, some of which were ad-libbed, weren't written until the writers interviewed each child and a "personality" was developed that matched who the child already was.

Unusual feat—the Silo spots ring very true, and that's the way both the advertiser and the agency wanted it. The people behind the campaign were sensitive to the special issues involved in using kids to promote adult products. Bruce Berkowitz, the senior account executive handling Silo's business at Lewis Gilman & Kynett, tells me about how they didn't want to make the kids into salespeople because they felt it was unnatural. As Mr. Berkowitz puts it, "Kids watch even though the target is adults, and it affects kids too." The key here is naturalness. But with kids in ads—as with adults—being natural rarely comes naturally. The ads are, of course, staged. The product has to be plugged. But there are some agencies that go out of their way to make sure they bring out the real kid in their child actors.

Not only can fake kids adversely reflect the trustworthiness of a brand; *faking* children's creations and passing them off in ads as being genuine kid productions can be turnoffs to adult consumers —whether or not the imitation is consciously recognized as such. The differences between the artwork or writing of a child and that of an art director trying to make the graphics *look* as if they were done by a child may appear negligible to the adult viewer at first glance, but at the level of awareness and memory where emotional responses function, the gaps are highly significant and unnerving.

We've all been children; at a subconscious level, we've all experienced the specific idiosyncrasies of drawing and writing that necessarily accompany immature emotional and visual-motor development. And if we have children, or know some personally, there's something disconcerting about being confronted with work that has been deliberately made awkward or sloppy by an adult so we'll think it's been done by a kid. The nagging uneasiness people sense with these art director–produced "child creations" stem also from a feeling that some form of insult is being done to the child—to the child in us all.

Gerry O'Hara, the art director at Ephron Raboy & Tsao, New York, is responsible for a superb use of genuine children's art in an ad for Boyd's, a men's clothing store in Philadelphia. Mr. O'Hara never even considered attempting to draw his concept himself. Boyd's prides itself on fitting big or tall men, and Mr. O'Hara imagined a child's perspective on size, shared through a drawing, could tell that story to shoppers in a uniquely engaging way. He got the idea from his five-year old daughter, who'd been drawing family-type pictures at home. He tells me he just asked her to "draw a picture of Mommy, Daddy, and you, but make Daddy really, really tall with long legs." Since he wanted the figures labeled, Mr. O'Hara wrote down the letters and had the little girl copy them. And he didn't correct them. The result, headlined "Good Things Come in Big and Tall Packages at Boyd's" is a positive attention-grabber. People tell the advertiser that it makes them feel good, and they comment on it when they come into the store to shop. That's a fair, although nonstatistical, estimate of advertising effectiveness. Why didn't this professional art director draw the family himself? Mr. O'Hara tells me, "I felt it should be done by an authentic artist." And he wasn't being funny. Authenticity doesn't just make psychological sense, it makes sales sense.

In contrast to the kinds of things that kids can actually create, kids who are called upon to fake the whole show look like sideshow shills. Consider Du Pont's ad for Stainmaster Carpet; a little boy is suited and bow-tied like a little man, as if he were an adult consumer. The ad, produced by Bunting Associates in Lancaster, Pennsylvania, tells readers to *Pick up the free book that tells you how to pick out your next carpet* and shows this tyke holding the booklet with an exaggerated "Oh, wow" expression on his face, perhaps in order to demonstrate the veracity of the copy's promise

that this free item is one "that'll open your eyes."

The Du Pont kid's contrived joyousness over a carpet catalog isn't the only counterfeit child-image in the ad. "Decorating Days" was apparantly written by a professional artist in multicolored, unevenly sized letters to make it look like a kid's printing. Maybe because I know how hard kids work to learn how to write, when I see an adult making letters deliberately too big, or clumsily, thinking they will represent the awkward writing of a child, it strikes me as condescending, a mockery of young efforts. And I don't believe for a minute that this is ever the advertiser's intent.

Ethical and psychological issues involved in using kids as commercial vehicles are highly complex and subtle. Often the difference between presenting a child in a natural, age-appropriate way and setting him or her up as an adult mouthpiece can come through just as clearly in nonverbal nuances, body language, voice tone, and clothing details as in verbal scripting.

If parents are pushing their offspring to achieve more, better, earlier; and if Madison Avenue models moppets in the high-speed lane of sales persuasion; and if kids (who always want to be older than they are) naturally try to emulate adult behavior, advertisers cashing in on kids have a responsibility to portray children *as* children. Advertisers do have the power to influence cultural expectations—negatively and positively. And as it turns out, when kids are allowed to be themselves in ads, the benefits to advertisers aren't just altruistic. In order to *buy*, consumers must *believe*. And no one is more believable than a kid who's just allowed to be a kid.

CHAPTER 9

STEREOTYPES BENEATH THE SKIN

Donna Weiss is a professional singer and songwriter who recently presented a program at The Miquon School, a small progressive school set in a woodsy Philadelphia suburb, where I spend some of my time consulting. Between songs, Donna told the children and adults gathered around her, in a completely matter-of-fact way, a little about herself.

Donna simply described, in detail, a variety of techniques and strategies she uses in order to go about her life as a blind person. She assumed the group's curiosity and revealed up front that she has a boyfriend, told us how she tells time by a talking clock, taught us about asking permission before petting *guide* dogs (*not* "Seeing-Eye," which is a *brand* name, and she prefers Second Sight). Throughout, Donna exuded a composed confidence.

Donna did not present herself as a person who had courageously overcome the challenge of her blindness, or as a person who had accomplished a great deal in spite of her disability. Donna presented herself as an intelligent, competent individual who considered being blind to be an unpleasant limitation that made it necessary for her to develop countless other means of acquiring information ordinarily available through vision. She didn't portray herself as either a victim or a victor; she portrayed herself as a person who needed to go through specific extra steps to do the same kinds of jobs that we all have to do.

Among other things, what struck me about Donna was the difference between how she portrayed herself and how most public-service advertising, and the media in general, portray a disabled person. By and large, PSA's, TV shows, and the press crank out pictures of the disabled population—when they appear at all—that boil down to a few standard, emotionally saturated stereotypes: Amazingly Accomplished Surmounters; Pitiable Victims of Fate; Courageous Copers. Donna was clearly uninterested in eliciting or shaping feelings; she was interested in being informative.

But Donna is a professional musician and seeks out the media for the same reasons as any other performer, and out of all the coverage she's been given, only one reporter focused so completely on her as a songwriter—and as a person—that he never even mentioned her disability. To the rest, she's been valiant, blind Donna, who also writes moving songs.

Mary Johnson publishes *The Disability Rag*, an iconoclastic journal, based in Louisville, Kentucky, which is highly influential in the growing disability-rights movement. It is radical in format (no heroic stories, no medical reports, no paid ads) and merciless in its jettisoning of stereotypes held not only by the general public, but by disabled people themselves. Her position is that "super-crips," who are implicitly or explicitly applauded for their achievements *in spite of* their disabilities, send a message about the unusualness of a disabled person accomplishing anything. The image of the handicapped hero as someone who pursues a normal, everyday goal, like getting a degree, implies that the disabled aren't really expected to do much in the world because of their pitiful limitations.

As I see it, the disability stereotypes wreak psychological havoc in a number of ways. On the one hand, images lionizing the "supercrip's" astounding feats give the general public a comforting excuse to continue to keep emotionally distant from the disabled: Focusing on their tremendous courage and specialness makes them all the more different from the rest of us. And most people are frightened of feeling too close to, or identifying with, the disabled, because they must then face their *own* vulnerability. On the other hand, this heroic imagery—featuring the one-legged athlete, the blind therapist, the quadriplegic scientist—sends the debilitating message to the great majority of disabled people that it's *not* okay to find their condition frustrating, tedious, and boring. Media images of people who do remarkable things in spite of their handicaps make it harder for the disabled to gain self-respect for themselves as they are—with aplomb—rather than having to constantly prove their bravery in the face of adversity.

When it comes to commercials directed to the general public, advertisers who use any images at all of disabled people are rare indeed. In fact, they're practically invisible. When members of a particular subgroup never see anyone who resembles them in ads —or in any of our culture's self-portraits—they get the message that they are nonpersons in the larger society. In their families or in their neighborhoods, they may be the greatest, but when it comes to participating in the images and symbols of success and happiness that are held up—rightly or wrongly—as cultural standards by advertising, they're nowhere to be seen. Even their money doesn't count, isn't solicited. In short, they don't exist.

Nissan is one of the few companies that have chosen to use a disabled person to advertise one of its products to the general public. I found Nissan's ad for its Stanza Wagon, created by Chiat/Day, in *Newsweek*—an unequivocally mainstream magazine—and was immediately struck by its psychological sensitivity, marketing savvy, and restraint. And when I asked the folks at *The Disability Rag* to send me any ads they felt good about, the only one I got was Nissan's.

Sally Wetzler, the woman featured in the Nissan ad, is a CPA. She was so impressed with what the Stanza's double sliding doors would allow her to do, that she got rid of her old full size, full-lemon, van (which needed a lift for her wheelchair) and bought the Nissan. She fell in love with it and thought that the company should know how she felt. She also thought that the company should direct its advertising for the Stanza toward the disabled population, which, as she put in her letter to Nissan, she felt represented an important market for the car.

Sally Wetzler drives a Stanza Wagon
for the same reasons other people do.
It's great for families, it carries a lot of
stuff, and it's easy to get in and out of.

Meet Sally Wetzler, a very nice woman in Richmond, Virginia,
who has some very nice things to say about her Stanza Wagon.

"I've been driving my Stanza for almost two years now, and
it's by far the best car I've ever owned.

"It's more economical than
my old van. It's a lot easier to
handle. But most important, the
two sliding doors make it totally accessible. I really feel as if
Nissan designed it for me."

Actually, it was designed for Sally Wetzler. And for everybody else who drives a family wagon.

For example, to make it easier to get in and out of, the Stanza
Wagon has sliding rear doors on both sides.

Because families need to carry a lot more than themselves,
the Nissan Stanza Wagon not only has fold-down seats so
you can really load it up, it also has a low cargo floor so you can
load it up easily.

And since most folks like to see where they're going, the
engineers at Nissan raised the roof and the driver's seat. For a
better view of the road.

It all comes down to Human Engineering. Which simply
means thinking about what a car is supposed to do for people.
All kinds of people. And then making sure it does it.

NISSAN

Built for the Human Race.

In response to Ms. Wetzler's comments, Nissan wrote that her letter had been passed on to the advertising agency. In response to her assumption that monster corporations would rather listen to themselves than to the consumer, Ms. Wetzler translated Nissan's reply as "Thank you for your thoughts; we've passed them on to the circular file." That was in October 1988.

In January 1989, Ms. Wetzler got a call from Patte Flaherty, Chiat/Day's account executive for Nissan, asking if they could use her in an ad to sell the Stanza—not just to the disabled market but to the general population—as part of the umbrella "Built for the Human Race" campaign. Ms. Wetzler agreed, but only on the condition that the ad not be patronizing. As it turned out, that condition had already been established by Nissan and Chiat/Day. No problem.

What's astonishing about the Stanza piece, beside the fact that one woman's articulate enthusiasm could have triggered such a significant response from a corporation, is that it uses a disabled person in a full-scale national ad in the same way that it would use anybody else—as just a person. In the ads, Ms. Wetzler talks about the particular reasons the Stanza is the "best car" she's ever owned. But she doesn't specifically refer to the car's accommo-dation of her wheelchair. In fact, there's no reference in the ad to her disability at all. Actually, she had to educate the people on the shoot about the realities of her disability; she refused to allow herself to be photographed at the top of a staircase, for example (even though she was assured that the stairs would be out of focus), because there was no wheelchair access.

As a marketing piece, the Nissan ad was quite successful. Ms. Wetzler personally handled a number of serious phone inquiries about the Stanza, some referred to her by the company and some from individuals tracking her down through the ad itself. As a stereotype-breaker, the ad was awarded and embraced by the disabilities community. There's so little of the kind of no-fanfare inclusion of a disabled person in consumer advertising that each time it occurs, it tends to be greeted by the media—and by the public—as being the first and only of its kind.

Back in 1984, Foote-Cone and Belding's advertising, developed for Levi Strauss & Company's 501 jeans, included a man in a wheelchair in one of its genuinely engaging, musically excellent, shamelessly imitated, sales-soaring "501 Blues" commercials. In the spot, young people are dancing, jogging, playing double-dutch— and here's this guy happily popping a wheelie in his chair—all to the sound of authentic blues. He's just another person having fun in his 501 jeans; he's defined by the personality he radiates, not by his disability. And his inclusion makes so much sense. Not only did the advertiser generate a positive human image of the disabled, it created a positive human image of itself. The benefits are mutual. Besides, what a smart way to sell

the product's promise of individuality, as delivered by the "501 Blues" song: "They shrink down to fit me,/so ya know what that means./It means I'm the only one/gonna fit in my jeans. . . ."

McDonald's and its ad agency Leo Burnett (of Volkswagen's classic "Lemon" ad) has integrated disabled people into a few commercials over the last several years. One particularly effective spot, "Silent Persuasion," showed a deaf boy successfully persuading a girl to take time off from studying for exams to grab lunch from a McDonald's and eat outside by the water, just like any other young couple more infatuated with each other than with Chemistry 101. The couple signed to each other throughout the subtitled commercial.

It's not the disabled who should be congratulated for their courageous overcoming of obstacles; it's the rare advertisers who dare to break two cardinal rules of stereotyping. First round of applause: those advertisers who present a disabled person as a regular member of the gang, the gang called the American public, instead of a sensational, or wretched, special case. Second round of cheers: those who go ahead and market their products to disabled people along with anybody else they'd try to get money out of, instead of either ignoring their wallets altogether, or imagining that they require uniquely targeted advertising in order to be convinced, for example, to eat hamburgers.

Nevertheless, for the most part the general public gets to see images of disabled people in PSAs and charity telethons, where they are trotted out as guilt-bait, and as examples of the horrible consequences of whichever disease the donations are supposed to cure. The plea is for contributions so that unfortunate little whoever in her darling ribbons and brave smile can one day throw away her braces, chair, crutches, and the like, forever. The message is that then, finally, the disabled will be just like us—the real people, the *normal* people. The psychological substrate of these stereotypical images, and of the need to eliminate signs of disability, or even to reject disabled people, stems more from the general population's *fear* of its own vulnerability than from hostility. Reminders of the existence of a disability in people *just like us*, not special or unique humans, cut pretty close to home for some, particularly for those who already feel vulnerable, or who are unconsciously afraid of becoming dependent themselves. For many people, stereotyping offers a cherished way to avoid getting too close for comfort. And stereotypes die hard.

In the spirit of trying to change the public's perception of disabled people, Smith Burke & Azzam, a Baltimore agency, recently created an unusual public-service TV campaign for the Maryland Council for Developmental Disabilities. In one spot, a handsome man, seated in a wheelchair, thanks the viewer for "the ramps on the curbs, the railings in the bathrooms," and other accommodations, but makes a specific request for another change: "Treat us like anyone else." This request for a change of attitude, rather than spare change, is unusual. But many disabled people have strong objections to the spot. The man in the chair was played by Joe Urla, a New York actor who was appearing off-Broadway at the time in *The Boys Next Door.* Mr. Urla is *not* disabled.

The Joe Urla spots generated a fair amount of controversy, and have a fascinating history. According to Katherine Hax, director of community education at the council, the original script had a different ending from the one that finally aired. In it, after Mr. Urla had thanked the public for all the nice ramps, he was supposed to say, while seated in the wheelchair, "Now, we'd like you to do one more thing. Don't treat us like *this;* treat us like *this,*" at which point he was to stand up. The idea was to counter the stereotype that viewers would presumably hold about the person in the wheelchair, by confronting them with the image of his being "just like anyone else without a disability."

It is doubtful that this well-meaning, but contrived strategy could have provoked the kind of shift in thinking its developers intended. More likely, it might have generated anger and confusion in viewers, which wouldn't do much to improve their perceptions of disabled people.

But the original ending was hotly debated by the council and eventually rejected, Ms. Hax tells me, as being demeaning, as denying the disability, as analogous to "telling people to treat a black person like they're white." Unfortunately, the decision *not* to have Mr. Urla stand up at the end of the spot came at the eleventh hour, when he was already under contract. Although he did a fine job of acting, the use of an able-bodied actor to portray a disabled person has stimulated negative reactions from the disabled community.

Regardless of Mr. Urla's contract, the majority of the council board members, which includes disabled people, felt that because the PSAs were to be targeted to the general population, and because Mr. Urla had impressed them with his acting skill, there was no compelling reason to select a disabled actor over one without a disability. The board felt that the casting should be done strictly on the basis of which actor could be most convincing and credible to the target audience. The general target audience, in this case, is one that has so little contact with disabled people that, presumably, it couldn't tell the difference—as long as Mr. Urla remained seated.

But *disabled* people can spot the differences between Mr. Urla and reality right away, and they've expressed anger that the council didn't give Mr. Urla's role to a disabled actor so that the positive message about treating disabled people "like anyone else" would be grounded in the reality of jobs—the put-your-money-where-your-mouth-is place. It's easy for a disabled person to spot the fact that Mr. Urla's chair has no cushion (which would always be there to prevent sores), that his feet aren't on the rests (where a bonafide user's would be), and that the chair is entirely too small for him. And they didn't like spotting these errors.

There's a story behind the wheelchair. The council is very pleased with the campaign, which has already won a creative award ("Baltimore's Best for PSAs"), and is very pleased with the agency, which has been extraordinarily helpful and capable. But the agency brought a wheelchair to the shoot, an old-fashioned youth chair, and that's the one they wanted to use. Even though Ms. Hax had brought along a nifty sport chair. The job needed to get done, and Ms. Hax is a diplomatic woman. She was diplomatic about the feet, too, the ones she thought should go on the footrests and that the agency figured would never show in the final editing.

These issues aside, Mr. Urla plays in two spots for the council. One of them leaps tall stereotypes in a single bound. In this spot, he sits there in his chair looking straight out at us and, without any introduction, starts to tell a joke, but in a very ordinary, very amateurish way. And as he fumbles toward the punch line, he takes a couple of stabs at it, and then forgets it completely. After he looks a little self-conscious, he says, "Hey, people with disabilities are only human." And then his voice trails off as he mutters to himself, "I should never tell jokes." This isn't a model of courage who, in spite of his handicap, went on to become a brilliant comedian! This is just a regular guy who told half of a dumb joke. Just the way anybody else could do.

Stereotypes die hard. And sometimes, as in the case of the elderly, people in our culture are terrified about facing the truth about a social group because, in doing so, they will have to face the truth about themselves. America worships youth and hates growing older; to Americans, aging means death, and we are terrified about dying. Coupled with the fantasy that if Americans consume perfect diets, aerobicize themselves into perfect bodies, and hem up their wrinkles into perfect faces, they will never get old and will never die, is disrespect for the power and knowledge of age. Much of America still thinks of itself as adolescent, a self-image that feeds the advertisers' own fantasies of youthfulness, which feeds the image-machines of advertising, which pumps up the measuring-up process, which validates the fear of aging. Where does it stop? It stops at the bottom line.

In the case of the elderly market, with its enormous buying power, advertisers have been making serious mistakes for years. And it's costing them a bundle. Recently, some advertisers have stood under the cold shower of reality long enough to wake up to the fact that they could lose staggering amounts of revenue if they don't learn how to connect with the mature consumer.

A friend and colleague of mine, George Gerbner, Ph.D., is the dean of the University of Pennsylvania's Annenberg School of Communications. Since 1967, he has directed an enlightening, ongoing study monitoring the relationship between people's television viewing and their perceptions of social reality. The Cultural Indicators Project's huge data bank reveals that people who are heavy viewers of television (over four hours a day) tend to see our society the way television tells them it is, which is often strikingly different from the real world. For example, the world of TV is one in which men outnumber women at least three to one; women are preoccupied with marriage, romance, and family, and are younger than the men they relate to; nonwhites are underrepresented victims; policemen and crime are omnipresent; doctors are omniscient. Television, taken as an aggregate of programming and commercials, tells the public that sixty-to-sixty-five-year-old people are getting sicker, poorer, and decreasing in number. Heavy viewers buy these images of the elderly as real. In fact, the exact opposite is true: Not only are most older Americans healthier and richer than ever before, they're swelling in numbers. And in terms of casting, older individuals are more likely to be found in comic than in serious roles. Old age is terrifying; it's easier to lampoon it than face it directly.

In Madison Avenue terms, we're looking at a fifty-plus age group that controls $130.3 billion in discretionary income, about 50 percent of the U.S. total. We're looking at 76 million baby boomers who will begin to retire in 2001. We're looking at advertising that reflects television's views of older Americans as a vanishing bunch of dotty fools, who are isolated from younger people and beset with financial and physical aches and pains. We're looking at a lucrative market with enough life experience to have their antennae exquisitely tuned to pick up condescending, insulting signals in ads. We're looking at people living off their savings and investments who have a strong disincentive to buy products that are useless or that represent them in humiliating ways.

Some advertisers have been paying attention to these developments and have scrambled to create images that counter obsolete stereotypes of older people. Some have scrambled so anxiously that the bad old stereotypes of the elderly as infirm, doddering dullards are being replaced by new, improved stereotypes of graying Americans, pumping away in exercise programs, filled with boundless energy and enthusiasm for life.

A few years ago, Eastern Airlines directed an ad to people sixty-two years old or older, created by Lintas: Campbell-Ewald, that it apparently intended as a compliment to its market. Ostensibly, the advertiser is telling older people that it sees them as vigorous sorts who have lots of living to do: The headline trumpets "A message for people who aren't content to travel just down memory lane." Seems positive enough at first glance, but underneath this

declaration lies an assumption that the advertiser unwittingly sends at the same time: Apart from these superior gray travelers, the rest of the older population, the *inferior* older population, is rocking away their memories on the porches of their lives. The dubious ploy of telling some consumers that they are more special than others doesn't cut it with the older population. Condescending to their *friends* is as quick a turn off as condescending to *them*. The elderly market is far more complex than advertisers portray. Why should reminiscing over beautiful memories be shameful?

Most older people are living better, feeling better about themselves, and are less willing than ever to listen to Madison Avenue tell them who they are if they don't like what they hear. And they're listening, and they're looking. There's an incongruous visual slip in the Eastern Airlines ad: The sturdy set of oldsters posed on the ridge of a mountain range, the paragons of get-up-and-go, are nattily attired (he in suit; she in skirt and heels), rather than wearing functional hiking clothes. Inadvertently, the advertiser has graphically buttressed the implied assumption that most old folks really do sit around and rock. A good chance to break the mold was only able to take off some chips. Why should the mature market believe that Eastern knows what aging really is about?

Fashion advertisers almost never have an older woman model anything, unless she's a celebrity like Linda Evans, Joan Collins, or Elizabeth Taylor. And these are women whose lives are devoted to the perpetuation of their public images, which must remain youthful at all costs, even when the price may include intermittent surgical "refreshments." Advertisers can get away with holding these sorts of mature women out to us because they appear to have been baptized in the Fountain of Youth, and so can assuage the general population's fear of aging. They tap into our need to measure up to the fantasy represented by such ageless, albeit Plasticine, models.

Market research, such as a survey sponsored by advertising agency Caldwell Davis Partners, New York, found that people over forty *feel* about fifteen years younger than their chronological ages, and that they tend to *see* themselves that much younger as well. I remember a sixty-five-year-old man commenting to me about how young he felt and how shocked he was looking in the mirror, thinking "Who's that?" With their association of feebleness with age, advertisers help create the disparity people perceive between their appearance and their sense of vitality. Advertisers adjust their imagery to match self-perceptions of older people that their advertising helped to instill. If the *norm* is that people feel about fifteen years younger than they look, perhaps it is *normal* for many wrinkled people to feel vital, energetic, and healthy. However, if media images tend only to associate vitality, energy, and health with unwrinkled models, the culture gives the message to older people that their feelings of vigor are somehow unnatural at their chronological age, that their feelings are really more appropriate for much younger individuals.

Naturally beautiful older women, with character in their faces and gray in their hair, are still largely disregarded as fashion models, even in an innovative magazine like *Lear's*, which positions itself "For the Woman Who Wasn't Born Yesterday." Although its features and departments intelligently examine relevant issues, and the lives of mature male and female leaders in their fields, young women like the minidress-sporting blonde in a recent issue model concepts like "We're big on the little white dress."

Nevertheless, *Lear's* does take a long-needed leap toward changing perceptions of sexuality in the older population. Although it's been no secret to psychological researchers and clinicians, as to advertisers for that matter, that older people like sex and romance, that reality continues to be virtually invisible in advertisers' imagery. But in the *Lear's* ad for media buyers, the handsome nude woman discreetly covering her breasts appears to have a healthy head of white hair—and looks confidently sexy. Sex and romance are very much alive in older people's relationships, but, with few exceptions, not when they look for themselves in Madison Avenue's family album. The McDonald's "Golden Time" spot, which features a budding romance between a charming elderly man and woman deciding to share a table at the restaurant, has been warmly received by the over-sixty-five set, but it stands out as an anomaly.

The reasons for the comparative invisibility of older people in ads, let alone older people in sexually suggestive situations, may be related to the existence of an unspanned generation gap: Many copywriters and art directors are under thirty. To advertising's creators, their perceptions of people old enough to be their parents, or even their grandparents, are colored by their relative youth, a psychological reality that could trigger unconscious fears and misunderstandings that leak out in stereotyped imagery, or motivate the *exclusion* of images of the mature population altogether.

Ironically, it is still difficult for most young adults to imagine that their parents have sex. I recall a friend of mine in graduate school telling me how uncomfortable he felt when he stayed with his parents over the holidays and could hear the sounds of their lovemaking through the walls of his room.

But facing up to a parent's sexuality is easy compared to facing up to what old age eventually leads to. It's emotionally safer to avoid being reminded of mortality by cutting images of older people out of advertising directed to the general population—even when they would fit naturally into the scene—or by creating stereotyped cartoons of the elderly so that the images don't feel so personally confrontive.

Nevertheless, as long as the profits of an advertising agency are tied into successfully reaching a target market, there's hope for change. That $130.3 billion bag of marbles the preretirement-but-getting-there market can decide to either play with or pack up and take home should begin to influence Madison Avenue's portraits of older America. Advertisers' artists need to improve their ability to capture true likenesses of these individuals, or they may find themselves with empty canvases and empty pockets. The older population has been around too long, has developed too strong a sense of identity, and has seen too much premium bull to sit still for a bad portrait.

Historically, while advertisers have tended to stereotype the elderly as feeble old fools, images of fat people of all ages are regularly stereotyped as lazy, babyish, stupid, and sloppy. Not too flattering.

I get a kick out of reading articles enthusiastically touting the New Voluptuousness in models, as if recent rerouting of fashion's flashlight from the rear to the breasts heralds a healthier, fleshier, idealized body. Not so. Thin remains American girls' Holy Grail of femininity, and they pursue it anxiously from grade school on. Lean models with this year's look in cleavage are still *lean*, and that's what American girls want to be—just as their big sisters and their mothers do. A 1983 poll of thirty-three thousand women who read *Glamour* magazine found that about 75 percent felt they were too fat, regardless of how much they weighed; more than half of the fourth grade girls surveyed in 1986 by *The Wall Street Journal* thought that they were too heavy. As far as the fabled rush to roundness goes, I helped design a 1987 survey of one thousand young women (the Caress Body BARometer Survey) that found that Jane Fonda's sinewy build was favored over Madonna's curves in a landslide win for thin.

Meagen is a fifth-grader who hates herself because she's too fat. She's a little plump, but so is her father, who thinks she's just fine the way she is. Meagen's slender mom is sincere and committed to helping Meagen feel better about herself, so she tries to praise Meagen for the strengths she has, like her skills in reading and playing the piano. Meagen's mom believes that she isn't bothered by her daughter's weight; she just wishes her husband would lose weight and tells him about it all the time. Meagen tells me that she hears all about her father being a "lazy pig," "garbage can," and "tubby hubby," but she assures me that it doesn't bother her. What really bothers Meagen is getting teased by a couple of kids at school. She's a friendly, bright little girl, and even though she has some friends, Meagen sees herself as fat, dumb, and unlovable.

Does Meagen ever get to see kids in ads for clothes or cereal or headphones or soda with even an ounce of excess adipose tissue? Not likely. Where Meagen *will* get to see herself portrayed is in the last pages of the magazine section of the Sunday papers—in the ads for fat camps. The rest of the advertisers—and the culture in general—send kids like Meagen the message that only the thin dance, have lots of friends, and wear cool clothes.

When they're used in ads at all, overweight kids are generally cast in extremely negative roles; they're slow or clumsy or clownish, which reinforces not only the prevailing cultural perceptions, but miserable self-concepts as well. Invariably, when I ask advertisers why they chose a fat kid to play a particular part in a commercial, they tell me it had nothing to do with his or her weight, that the child was cute or photogenic or somehow just seemed right. Nobody likes to admit—even to himself—that he stereotypes.

Some years ago, Edwin Bird Wilson, Inc., created an ad for Corroon & Black, a business insurance firm, which pictured a bright, alert, *thin* class, each student straining a raised hand to get called on—eager beavers all. All except one, that is. The fat boy right smack in the front with his arms folded has the wide-eyed

Risk. There is no substitute for knowledge.

You can't get intelligent risk management solutions without asking intelligent questions. That's how we feel. So we offer our clients a unique perspective of the risks they face. Utilizing the kind of technological and human resources that you'd expect from us, one of the world's largest insurance brokers. It's this full-service approach to business insurance that has served our clients successfully for over 75 years. Wherever in the world they do business. So, contact us. We'll give you the answers, not excuses.

CORROON & BLACK
Putting insurance risks into perspective.
Wall Street Plaza, New York, N.Y. 10005 · 212-363-4500

look of a kid who didn't do his homework and is praying with every cell in his body that the teacher won't call on him. On his desk is the telltale sign of a lazy goof-off—a paper airplane. Putting aside the oddity of the advertiser's symbolically telling its business market that answers to its risk-management questions will be provided by a bunch of grade-school kids, the decision to cast an obese little boy as the class dummy didn't just happen because he could create such a convincing caught-off-guard look. Imagine what a set-breaker it would be if one of the kids with stereotypically brainy glasses were cast as the school slouch and the big guy in the front were in there flapping his arm at the teacher with the right answer!

Commodore-Amiga, Inc., didn't. The advertiser stayed stuck in the same old stereotype as Corroon & Black. Its ad for Amiga Computers ran a few years after Corroon & Black's, but looks just like it. This time, though, the fat kid is plopped in the middle of the class—every other one of whom is again desperately seeking salvation in a chance to blurt out the right answer (they're the ones who have Amigas at home). This time, though, the fat kid looks more sheepish and is resting his chin on his upstretched thumb—a thumb that is precariously close to his mouth. This time, the fat kid represents the babyish, rather than the lazy, stereotype. Commodore-Amiga's strategy in this ad is similar to the advertiser's message in the "Train" commercial, the one where Junior flunks out of college because Mommy and Daddy didn't buy him a computer. Junior, the loser in "Train," is also fat.

A few years ago, Subaru ran a spot, created by Levine, Huntley, Schmidt & Beaver, Inc., that featured a group of boys playing touch football in the street as a device for showing how unrecognizably different one of its newest models had become from the public's perception of a Subaru sedan. One of the handsome, all-

American, blond, athletic—thin—young boys tells the only fat kid in the huddle about a play that will involve his receiving a pass by the Subaru parked up the street. As the playing begins, the fat boy is shown looking confused, and bumbling around literally in circles as he attempts to find the Subaru, at which point the football is passed to him and hits him in the chest. Why does the fool have to be *fat?* Because he was photogenic. At least that's what I was told.

A truly bright spot in the bleak collection of images of the overweight in advertising is one that ran in the Marriott Corporation's "What A Taste" campaign for Roy Rogers's restaurants not long ago. There, surrounded by an otherwise slender group, is an attractive heavy woman dancing skillfully along with the others, not as a stereotype of the fat-and-happy sort, but as an equal member of the group. And she's enjoying Roy's *fried chicken* along with the others; she's not judiciously nibbling lettuce in obeisance to the cultural god of Svelte.

Why are overweight kids and adults scorned? One of the collective fantasies of American culture, of the American Achievement Machine, is that we are in control of our lives. We believe that perseverance, determination, and assertiveness—inborn, or acquired through training courses for a small fee (small in light of promised renewed earnings capacity)—will get us what we want and where we want to go. We can do anything, we are told, if we *want* to do it badly enough. The catch? If we slow down or, the unthinkable, *stop,* the fear is that the Achievement Machine will lose its momentum and we will regress. Fat people aren't perceived as achievers; unconsciously, they're seen as people who *can't* control themselves, as people whose lives center around eating, like babies. Psychologically, overweight people symbolize the regression that people in this culture are so afraid of in themselves. Instead of facing their own wishes to take it easier rather than treadmilling toward heaven, or to indulge in delicious food rather than analyzing each bite's longevity quotient, those desperate to be slim, desperate to be successful, stereotype overweight people (including themselves) as lazy good-for-nothings.

Roseanne Barr, the fat-and-proud-of-it star of television's *Roseanne* has thundered into the popular culture as a brash, confident, hard-working woman in a physically affectionate, warmly jousting marriage with an equally fat man. One media character isn't about to transform America's collective unconscious, but the public seems to love Roseanne, and her undaunted ego presents a positive image of one of America's favorite scapegoats. Although *Roseanne* is actually unearthing the jolly fat-lady stereotype, there's one critical difference: Ms. Barr projects a rocklike sense of security, and I believe that's what people are warming up to in her character. Not bad as a model for overweight people, especially women, to measure up to. Not bad as a model for *advertisers* to measure up to.

Stereotypes *can* be changed, if not eliminated. Given weak sales or enough consumer pressure, Madison Avenue will give second thoughts to what it's saying about people through the communication symbols in its ads. When the heat is on, ad directors can become acutely sensitive to the ways they might be turning off, rather than turning on, their potential audience.

Stereotypes of ethnic minorities in particular have come a long way, largely in response to public pressure. What made the biggest difference, of course, was concerted pressure from black groups and outspoken individuals who wouldn't stand for the crass stereotyping that pervaded magazines through the fifties. It's interesting to see how quickly advertisers began to self-consciously improve their acts once the ante was upped. While they may be at a bit of a loss right now in knowing how to bring their message to a fully multiracial, multiethnic audience, it seems safe to say that advertisers are sensitized to the basic issues. While they're making gaffes, at least they're *trying* not to be offensive.

To note the contrast, all we have to do is look at the bad old days. American ads from the first half of the twentieth century used images of blacks that reflected their subservient stations in life—such as servants, porters, field hands —and caricatured them as loafers, or buffoons, or jokesters. An early ad, which in the late nineteenth century took the form of a trade card, promoted the powerful cleansing properties of the advertiser's soap by showing a black being transformed into a Caucasian by being washed with the product.

The story of the evolution of Aunt Jemima's image provides a condensed picture of the changes in the use of blacks in advertising over the years. Aunt Jemima's roots began in the 1890's, when she was depicted as a renowned cook—and also as a former slave. In 1924, in a *Ladies' Home Journal* ad where she appears in a stereotypical "mammy" form (round-faced, kerchiefed, grinning), the copy refers to her life on the old plantation. The ad changed, but the message was essentially the same for the next twenty years. In a 1943 *Life* ad, Aunt Jemima appears to be more of a servant, complete with expressions like

AUNT JEMIMA PANCAKE FLOUR

"folks sho' whoops with joy . . ." Understandably, during the 1960's civil rights era, the image of Aunt Jemima was held out and hated by blacks as a repugnant stereotype. Until quite recently, Aunt Jemima's current image had been relegated to a small oval in the corner of the package and showed a younger, modern African-American housewife with a checkered headband substituting for the kerchief. Currently, Aunt Jemima now sports pearl earrings and

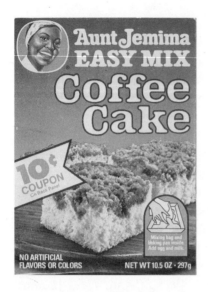

no head covering over her stylish, gray-streaked hair. She is very much a contemporary woman.

Aunt Jemima may have come a long way, but where is advertising in terms of its use of blacks today? It's hard to tell. The CEBA—Communications Excellence to Black Audiences—awards should provide some guidelines in answering that question, but the issues surrounding what constitutes great ads using blacks are confusing even to those on the inside track. Although Ogilvy & Mather's campaign using Ray Charles as a celebrity card-holder was a 1988 CEBA winner, CEBA judges and past judges debate whether such casting is tokenism, or whether highlighting one of its most successful members makes much impact on African-American consumers as people.

When I saw the Ray Charles piece, I thought about a public-service ad I saw some years ago, put out by BOCA—the Black Owned Communications Alliance. In it, a young black boy, chest out, caped in a towel, faces his bathroom mirror and sees the reflection of a white Superman. Underneath this image is the question "What's wrong with this picture?" The copy answers itself: "Plenty, if the child is Black and can't even *imagine* a hero the same color he or she is."

Psychologically, it *is* important for positive superheroes like Bill Cosby, Ray Charles, and Whitney Houston to be advertised in the general media along with Jell-O and Amex and Coke. It's especially important for black kids developing a sense of who they are and who they can become, not just in the African-American community but in the broader culture as well. But when pictures of superheroes, such as athletes, dominate images of blacks in

advertising, unconscious stereotypes can become even more entrenched. An ad for Kenzo
designer clothing sends a rather
insidious message about blacks
that combines both damaging
stereotyping with poor taste in a
print piece in which nobody comes
out ahead of the game.

What's wrong with this picture?

The Kenzo ad makes use of
the popular creative strategy of
visually conveying both sides of
the target's assumed "split personality" in order to demonstrate
the product's ability to integrate
effectively with all parts of the "real" person.

BOCA The Black Owned Communications Alliance
P.O. Box 2757 Grand Central Station, New York, New York 10017

As the Kenzo ad is structured visually, the symbolic messages
are quite different from what is stated in the small copy block.
The page is dominated by the deadly serious figure of the black

boxer, gloves ready, muscles taut.
The foppy-looking guy in the cute
bow tie and plaid trousers standing in the box (ring?) at fist level
comes across just like the kind of
character the Red Gloved War-
rior would love to flatten just for
looking like such a wimp.

What the copy hopes we'll
understand, however, is that the
Kenzo Kid is not a wimp at all,
but has simply "left conformity
behind him." Furthermore, the
boxer is supposed to actually be
a vision of the "inner man" be-

neath the plaid getup. Now, this kind of psychological stereotyping
does nobody very much good. The message to the unconscious is
that aggression is a black man (a doubtlessly unintended bit of
racial stereotyping) and that Kenzo consumers seethe and ripple
under their mild-mannered exteriors. In terms of marketing im-

pact, this is a psychological message that the designer's target audience might not want to hear.

If there is little real integration of black and white imagery in the general media, then the mirror will continue to reflect the disenfranchisement and disillusionment of African-Americans in this country. During Black History Month, advertisers fall all over each other trying to prove how meaningfully they can relate to black consumers. For the most part, though, their earnest approaches to the black market are published exclusively in black media like *Essence* and *Ebony* magazines. I wish a wonderful print ad, produced internally by Polaroid Corporation, had appeared in general-public as well as black-targeted magazines during Black History Month in 1989. The ad shows a 1948 snapshot of three little boys, one black and two white, subheaded "Small wonders, big dreams." It's warm, unpretentious, unselfconscious —and took place before the civil-rights movement.

African-Americans are certainly not the only ethnic minority to have gone through advertisers' image-grinders and emerged in

unflattering, lopsided cartoon shapes. In terms of its effect on ethnic identities, utilizing a stereotyped image doesn't *necessarily* make an ad damaging. What gets people upset—and rightly so—is when advertising promotes *negative* stereotypes. From early caricatures of the rough, rumpled immigrant laborer as lacking in proper manners and proper language, evident in a 1933 sheet-music cover: "I break-a da stones/ So I can make-a da mon/To give a da wife/To put in-a sock/For

Saturday night," Italian-American stereotypes in ads fall into two major groups today. On the one hand, we have the Italian momma busily feeding her brood, favored by spaghetti-sauce advertisers like Ragù. On the other hand, we see the smooth, seductive Italian like the urbane fellow in a Bandolino campaign that ran a few years ago.

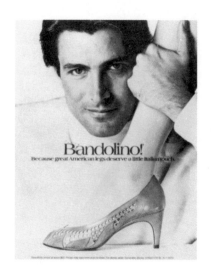

Actually, the Bandolino ad plays on two stereotypes at the same time: number one, Italian men are sexy, and two, American women have "great legs." Both are reasonably positive images. The ad's psychological and sales effectiveness are heightened by having the leg visible only from midcalf down, a perspective from which most women's legs look pretty good, even "great." This makes it easy for women to project themselves into the fantasy of having the kind of legs that "deserve a little Italian touch."

But there's another ethnic stereotype that is borne by Italian-Americans, which movies and television have used to bolster their profit margins for many years: the gangster—the mafiosi. But could it sell spaghetti?

Kirshenbaum & Bond thought it could. That's the same ad agency that signed up Donna Rice as the spokesperson for No Excuses jeans during the Gary Hart scandal.

Positano is a classy Italian restaurant in New York City that wanted to make a name for itself with the avant-garde, to be known as a relaxed, casual, trendy place. Enter Kirshenbaum & Bond, whose explicit marketing strategy for their first year in business (which began midway through 1987) was, according to Jonathan Bond, "to draw as much attention to ourselves as we could." Good or bad—notice us.

And, of course, notice our client. The ad Kirshenbaum & Bond created for Positano did what it was designed to do. It got noticed. The bullet-hole-riddled ad, dominated by the words "An Authentic Italian Restaurant Where No One's Been Shot. Yet" ran

AN
AUTHENTIC
ITALIAN
RESTAURANT
WHERE
NO
ONE'S
BEEN
SHOT.

YET

in *Detail* and *Spy,* two decidedly out-of-the-mainstream, irreverent magazines read by the hot young trendsetters Positano coveted. If these cognoscenti were moved to bless Positano with their presence, the restaurant could make it with the downtown crowd. They were so moved, and many authentic Italian meals were sold after the ad ran. And Kirshenbaum & Bond got lots of attention, which makes sense, at least in part, because the agency and the advertiser are looking for raves from similar reviewers—the young and the outrageous.

But outside of its specialized target, the Positano ad got panned. The restaurant, run by Italians, received enraged letters from Italian-American patrons and others decrying the ad's mob references. Bob Giraldi, one of Positano's co-owners, had been an art director at Young & Rubicam and did the art direction on the ad. According to him, some people the ad offended claimed they'd never come back to Positano because, as one put it, "After all the years we tried to play down the mob and Mafia connection, the ad fueled the fire."

Win some, lose some.

Some people can't take a joke. The advertiser wasn't seriously promoting the association of murder, death, and Italians. As Kirshenbaum & Bond point out, "The ad is tongue-in-cheek. Positano is an Italian restaurant that can laugh at itself." The guffaws must have subsided rather abruptly, since the advertiser withdrew the ad after running it only once. Nevertheless, Positano is delighted with its agency's work. It broke into the rarefied ranks it sought. But to many native Italians, or Italian-Americans, this "authentic Italian restaurant" sold its soul—and a piece of theirs—for the sake of pasta profits.

More and more, advertisers have had to become sensitized to the problems both of presenting homogenized images of people in order to capture a broader mass market, and of trotting out warmed-over—or souped-up—ethnic stereotypes in an effort to reach specific segments of the market. If nothing else, advertising pays homage to the bottom line. As consumers have become increasingly sophisticated and self-confident, they have grown less willing to buy products if they don't accept the images of themselves and of the people they love that are used as advertising vehicles. This is the era of the consumer's revenge, and advertisers are listening with all due respect.

CHAPTER 10

AD SPACE: IS THERE A FINAL FRONTIER?

If I'd written this book fifty years ago, it would have talked only about print advertising. Writing this book today, I looked at broadcast as well as print. And if I'd written it fifty years from now, what new media would I have had to include?

Advertising expands, and will continue to expand, to invade every imaginable communication avenue. Most of us still remember the days when the credit-card bill just told us what we owed. Now, a statement is an incidental in a stack of advertising inserts. Today, people pay outrageous prices for clothing that turns them into walking billboards for companies like Coca-Cola. We sighed a collective sigh of relief and blessed modern technology when cable TV offered us continuous sponsor-free viewing until the inevitable commercial encroachment began. Commercials custom-designed to fit with particular movies appear on videotapes, and studies find that most of us *don't* zap through them. Look for commercials coming to a theater near you; Coke is testing consumer reactions to movie spots as I write. And there is a company out there, right now, making profits selling advertising space on the inside of stall doors in public toilets.

E.T. didn't just happen to like Reese's Pieces and foster a national feeding frenzy of the little candies (resulting in a 65 percent increase in sales after the movie came out); advertisers pay huge sums to have their brands heralded by Hollywood. Product placement, the paid insertion of name-brand products in movies, is big business in the advertising industry. As clutter and cynicism increase, advertisers crank up their efforts to create messages about products that cannot be immediately identified as advertising. Having movie stars incorporate various brands into their characters' lives creates the illusion of natural preference rather than artificial sell. But assiduous effort and attention to detail on the part of a product-placement *specialist* goes into the fabrication of a "natural" yet highly visible role for the brand.

In *Moonstruck*, for example, not only does Cher's character order Mumm champagne, the shopkeeper keeps the bottle fully facing the audience. Seagram's, Mumm's parent company, paid fifty thousand dollars for the brand's subtle advertising messages in the film, and considers it to be an extremely valuable investment. Every chance to place products in a movie is carefully explored by specialists on a scene-by-scene, page-by-page basis. And each year, virtually all major consumer-goods companies are offered hundreds of placement opportunities. *Big* business.

Product placement in movies has gotten to be such a pervasive and disturbingly subtle behemoth that consumer watchdogs, such as the Center for Science in the Public Interest, have marshaled an attack on the practice. The center is calling for product placements to be either banned altogether or disclosed by announcing them, perhaps along with the movie credits, to clarify that a particular brand's presence is, in effect, a paid advertisement.

Ethical and marketing issues aside, artistic considerations made the existence of the product-placement industry plausible. In light of the sophistication of today's audiences, generic bottles labeled "Soda" would be likely to interrupt a film's credibility. But is this a strong enough argument to convince consumer activists to back off? The jury is still out. Meanwhile, advertising and movie moguls are sweating, and people like Michael Jacobson, executive director of the Center for Science in the Public Interest, are counting. To be exact, in *Bull Durham*, the baseball-movie hit, Mr. Jacobson counted fifty product mentions. Entertainment and advertising are blending.

In print and television, the lines between programming and editorial content are also becoming increasingly blurred. Recently, a series of fifteen- and thirty-second Ragù spots were created by the advertiser's agency, Waring & La Rosa, a small New York shop, with input by Bill Persky, producer of CBS's *Kate & Allie*, which looked for all the world like miniature sitcoms. They feature the De Luca family, a laugh track, and canned applause. The spots, shot on a sitcom set in a sitcom kitchen on sitcom tape, are so realistically unreal—or unrealistically real that they sneak right by until the product identification for spaghetti sauce appears at the end. The sitcom campaign is designed (the advertiser hopes) to be zap-proof. Meaning, Ragù hopes that people will sit still long enough to watch for example, a mother-in-law follow "an old Italian custom" of bringing her own spaghetti sauce (yes, Ragù, big studio laugh and applause) when she comes to stay with her son and his family. Ragù's Old World slice-of-life nostalgia spots are no longer running; maybe they still set off too many commercial-warning systems.

Sitcom spots relate to TV in the same way that advertorials— ads that look like articles—relate to magazines. Advertorials are a hybrid of advertising and quasi-editorial content that can easily be mistaken for part of the regular magazine materials. Typically, they are designed to mimic the publication's style in terms of typeface, tone, and content. When even *The New Yorker*, a long standing holdout to such tactics, accepts advertorials, *caveat emptor!* In a self-regulatory effort, the American Society of Magazine Editors has established guidelines that include having the word "advertising" written on each page of an advertorial. What happens when the guideline is routinely disregarded? Breathe easy, consumers— a warning letter is sent to the offending advertiser.

What else is new? It's advertiser-produced network programs —in a giant leap backward to the 1950's and 1960's, when such shows as *Hallmark Theater* were regulars in TV's early years. Advertisers like Clorox Company, which recently produced "Memories Then and Now," get to call the shots on program content and air their names every time the show itself is advertised. And while it airs? No clutter, no contest. All the commercials are Clorox's.

But what happens when programming developed by advertisers isn't designed for network television, but for the classroom? To run nationally? Chris Whittle, head of Whittle Communications, is concerned about the level of cultural illiteracy in American's schools. Mr. Whittle has created Channel One, which is currently being tested in high schools across the United States. Channel One is an entertaining program of national news, which Whittle Communications beams directly into the schools themselves, which are provided with color TV monitors, VCRs, and satellite dishes by the company. And the schools get to use the electronic equipment any way they like. The hitch? In exchange for all that neat stuff, the ten-minute news program is required daily viewing for the students—and it includes a full two minutes of commercials. Of course, Whittle Communications maintains that the spots will be in good taste and that they must pass the school's standards of acceptability. Of course, the appropriateness of *any* such commercialization of the classroom is being fervidly debated. Can textbooks with ads be far behind? It's everywhere, and it's in places we haven't even thought of yet.

Which raises two questions. First of all, do we always know what advertising *is?* And second, do we have the critical powers to understand what advertising is doing to us?

As advertising becomes more pervasive, it may also become less conspicuous. We're all familiar with the obvious tie-ins between advertised products and editorial matter in magazines. Fashion magazines are most blatant. Models dress up in the advertisers' dresses, shoes, lipstick, and pose for a section about this season's styles, colors, and fashions. The creator or manufacturer of the product is, of course, given credit. In fact, it's more than likely that the advertiser will buy a page or two in the same issue. In the glossy pages of *Vogue* or *Elle*, it all blurs harmlessly together. Between ads and magazine-photo-features, readers get their fill of fashions, and the cozy relationship between magazine advertisers and magazine publishers is happily maintained. Conflict of interest—or, rather, overlap of interest—is a trivial issue. If some reader mistakes an ad for a feature, or a feature for an ad, who cares?

But the situation is somewhat different when, for instance, a political advertisement written in the form of an editorial appears in a nationally circulated newspaper or a political-commentary magazine. The publisher demands that the boldfaced headline—ADVERTISEMENT—appear at the top of the paid-for-by-someone "editorial," and often, this type of ad is further set off by a defined border around the outside. Clearly, the publisher does not want readers to think that a paid-for political advertisement represents the views of the magazine.

But what distinction does the *reader* make? To exaggerate, if a newspaper were half editorials and half paid-for political advertisements, would the casual reader remember which was which? Would the "facts" in the paid-for advertorial be less credible than the "facts" expressed in the "Editor's Opinion" column? As advertising becomes more invasive, our opinions are increasingly shaped by it. And I doubt that, were no sponsor mentioned, even the most discriminating reader could separate paid-for opinions from un–paid-for opinions.

If this seems like too much worry over too small a distinction, we should pause for a moment to consider how children will separate the "news" in the Whittle Communications programs from the "product news" that they'll be getting at the same time, through the same medium, in the classroom. The message to students when a teacher turns on a video in the classroom is "This is something you should know about." When that video shows commercials, is the teacher saying, "You should know about these new products, along with the other news of the week"?

Unless they make their own value judgments, kids are likely to take it all as "news." And on a psychological level, adults are not much more sophisticated in their receptivity than kids are, because visual imagery is processed so immediately, so emotionally, for all of us. Which makes the stronger statements about George Bush—his paid-for revolving-jail-door commercial or his statements during an interview? Most viewers, I think, would make a distinction between the more emotionally based commercial and the more rational interview. But when it comes voting time, the intellectual distinction may be considerably less important than the emotional impact. If it's the *commercial,* rather than the interview, that gets people to vote for George Bush, the lesson is that the distinction between what is a paid-for political ad and what *isn't* is becoming increasingly obscured.

As advertising has invaded fashion and politics, it has also invaded every facet of the entertainment industry. Commercials can now use the best film directors, actors, and cinematography to create watchable—often wonderful—miniature movies. In some instances, we have already reached the point where the quality of commercials outshines the quality of entertainment offered side by side on the same network. Meanwhile, recording artists have made the crossover. In the "Michael Jackson" commercials for Pepsi, the product was almost a background sponsor for the entertainers. When you drank your Pepsi, you not only supported the advertiser, you also helped to ensure that *next year's* hot recording star would be tapped to provide thirty-second entertainment spots (compliments of Pepsi) during *next year's* Super Bowl. But when Pepsi picked Madonna, the choice turned out to be too hot to handle. The $5 million campaign featuring the extravagantly sexy vocalist had to be scrapped because of its links to Madonna's highly controversial "Like a Prayer" music video.

In this context of pervasive advertising, the question is bound to arise: Who (or what) buffers us from its influence? There's not much. There are, of course, truth-in-advertising practices, and an advertiser can be scolded, fined, or sued for blatantly false representations. The media, too, authorizes a certain number of constraints of varying degrees. Some publications will reject ads that are deemed less than tasteful, and some newspapers and magazines set standards for paid political ads that appear on their pages. And the networks set criteria related to content such as nudity and obscenity in commercials. But for the most part, advertising comes to us without screening of any kind. There's no plain brown wrapper around Obsession ads or a "PG-13" rating on ads for toy machine guns. The psychological screening is all up to us. We can look at it or look away, ignore or buy, sneer or laugh, believe or disbelieve. But will we?

This lack of screening has caused some advertising observers to become watchful and cautious to the point of paranoia. They warn of hidden messages. We are told (occasionally) that Madison

Avenue conspires to feed us distortions that subliminally prey upon our vulnerabilities. But the "Big Brother" image of Madison Avenue is vastly distorted. The advertising world is, without question, engaged in a massive, all-consuming scramble to sell goods, ideas, images, and entertainment. But manipulative is an insufficient description of this scramble. It's also desperate. Desperate to grab our attention, hold it (if only for a few seconds), and get across the message before it's buried under an avalanche of conflicting and contradictory clutter and other messages.

But if we have no external screen from the impact of advertising, and if the lines between advertising and other forms of communication are becoming even more obfuscated, what saves us from being swamped, duped, or molded by paid-for announcements?

Nothing, I believe, except our critical powers. And this is where, I also believe, more can be done to deal effectively with the reality of advertising rather than cursing its pervasiveness.

The irony here is that advertisers *can* be very critical about themselves, but a large amount of that self-alertness may never reach the vast audience of viewers, readers, or listeners who ingest advertising in enormous quantities. *Advertising Age* and *Adweek*, the pair of trade publications that are read religiously by most people in the industry, have their own acerbic, no-holds-barred critics who willingly make observations about the industry. *Advertising Age*'s current critic-in-residence, Bob Garfield, has a column with a movie-review format. He awards stars, ranging from four, for a top-of-the-line ad, down to one star, for "Pathetic efforts." Barbara Lippert provides a similar voice at *Adweek*. These are writers, not market researchers, and they don't show any special respect for the industry or its gurus. But it's the industry that peruses, and critiques, these critics.

What's curious, and perhaps significant, is that, with some exceptions, such as *The Village Voice*, which runs a regular feature critiquing ads, very few such critics write for the popular press. And why not? The audience certainly is there. We're all part of it. Many of us spend more time with advertising than we do with books, music, art, or film. Ads influence what we eat, what we wear, what we drive, whom we elect. But outside the trade journals, ads go largely unscrutinized.

What we have to keep in mind is that most of our media is

advertising-supported. A critic who questions the veracity of an ad's claims or pops the bubble of its pretenses or analyzes its persuasive strategies just might be shooting his rich uncle in the foot. Publishers may privately decline to accept an ad of questionable taste, but they do not enlist critics to comment on the ads that do appear. Books, movies, dance, art, theater, get critiqued throughout the popular media. Advertising—far more prevalent than any of these "higher" art forms—usually doesn't. In a way, this is all part of the process of saying that it doesn't really exist, doesn't really influence us, or doesn't really matter.

But it *does* matter. Advertising shapes egos, influences our sense of self-worth. It reinforces our fears that we never have enough; we're never healthy enough, good-looking enough, or lively enough. Advertising provides us with entertainment and, along with that, fantasies. It feeds our wishes, profits from our illnesses, plays on our insecurities, cautions us, exhorts us, reminds us of our past and future, and encourages us to behave in ways we have never behaved before. No one should be panicked by the thought of advertising's influence. It does, of course, have limits. But when it begins at an early age and follows us through our lives, we should at least be critically aware of what's happening.

I am not advocating that advertising critics be hired, *en masse*, by the popular media. On the other hand, I believe the hour is long overdue when we should develop a critical language to help describe the way advertising affects us. It's a powerful psychological and economic force, a dominant industry. Its power in the culture and in our lives is part reality and part myth, and one way to dispel and unravel its power is by pointing at where it works and where it doesn't.

Of course, we can judge advertising solely by the standards of entertainment. Once a year, the Siskel and Ebert movie critic team is hired by *Advertising Age* to do just that—to entertain—at their creative workshops. They watch a lot of commercials and give their opinions *just* on the quality of the film or video. But that's not the end of the road for an ad: An advertisement that is not very effective as entertainment may be *very* effective in getting people to buy a particular product—and hence have a run that far outdistances whatever entertainment value it may have. Conversely, an ad that gets a four-star rating on any critic's entertainment scale may be a one-star dud as far as selling product is concerned.

Advertising is always a battle of psychological wits. It wants us to *do* something. It wants us to buy. And its "success" lies in its ability to get us to believe in the fantasy and then take that next step. Its "success" lies in its effects on our decision-making. Familiarity with the ways of advertising may breed contempt; it's quite easy, nowadays, to find people who say they know what advertising is all about, and who laugh at the antic methods used by advertisers to influence people. But advertising is far too complex—and too powerful—to be summarily dismissed by scorn.

Critical understanding of advertising needs to keep pace with advertising itself. This is a significant challenge. As advertisers vie for attention, they also vie for innovation. The next assault on our senses is nearly impossible to predict. The best we can do, given the inevitable economic movements of advertising, is to acknowledge and understand how it's influencing us, why it's trying to influence us that way, and then attempt to separate ourselves from the images, and act objectively. That's our personal yardstick in the mutual measuring-up game we all play with Madison Avenue.

INDEX